CONSERVATORY STYLE

Garden Rooms, Glasshouses,
and Sunrooms

Jackum Brown

CONSERVATORY STYLE

Garden Rooms, Glasshouses, and Sunrooms

Universe

For my mother, Ursula Hoare, who loves plants

First published in the United States of America in 2007 by
Universe Publishing
A division of Rizzoli International Publications, Inc.
300 Park Avenue South
New York, NY 10010
www.rizzoliusa.com

Originally published in Great Britain as
Conservatories and Glasshouses in 2006 by
Mitchell Beazley
an imprint of Octopus Publishing Group Ltd
2–4 Heron Quays, London E14 4JP

Commissioning Editor: Michèle Byam
Art Editor: Victoria Burley
Senior Editor: Peter Taylor
Copy Editor: Anne McDowall
Design: Tim Harvey
Production: Angela Young
Proofreader: Clare Peel
Index: Sue Farr

ISBN-10: 0-7893-1521-1
ISBN-13: 978-0-7893-1521-2
Library of Congress Control Number: 2006923666

2007 2008 2009 2010 / 10 9 8 7 6 5 4 3 2

Printed and bound in China by
Toppan Printing Company Limited

Contents

Introduction

The desire to grow and enjoy tender and exotic trees and plants has been with us for hundreds of years. It is part of human nature to strive for knowledge about the world in which we live and to make the most of all that we discover.

By the beginning of the 16th century, fleets of ships were transporting materials from the empire-building countries of Europe – the Netherlands, France, Germany, and England – to Asia, Africa, and the Americas. The ships returned home laden with exotica that included new plant species, as well as herbs and spices, and existing European gardens of medicinal plants were enthusiastically augmented with the new discoveries.

Citrus fruits – oranges, in particular – were especially popular, but it was immediately obvious that these plants, like others from warmer climates, needed to be protected from European winter conditions if they were to survive and prosper. The first "orangeries" were built in the Netherlands of stone, brick, and wood and were heated by stoves. Over time, other plants, such as pomegranate trees, myrtles, and passionflowers, joined oranges and lemons and were cultivated in what became known as "greenhouses".

For a period during the mid-17th century, neither England nor Germany was well placed to develop greenhouse culture, which was the domain of the nobility and the extremely wealthy. While Germany was attempting to recover from the Thirty Years' War, England was in the grip of Oliver Cromwell and the Puritans, who frowned upon such ostentatious displays of wealth. France was ruled by Louis XIV, the Sun King, legendary for his extravagant living – despite growing social and economic problems in his country at that time. Louis loved to create new palaces and hunting lodges for himself, and considered the surrounding grounds to be as important as the buildings. His major project was at Versailles, and work on the park, including commissioning the first orangerie within it, began about five years before the renovation of the château itself. Louis XIV was enormously influential, and accounts of his fabulous gardens and orangeries soon spread all over the civilized world.

In the late 17th century in England, King William III (William of Orange) and Queen Mary, who were very interested in gardening, commissioned the first royal greenhouse to be built at Hampton Court Palace. Lord Capel of Tewkesbury had two greenhouses added

ABOVE **This spectacular raised conservatory joined two buildings in Paris. The illustration comes from Victor Petit's** *Parcs et Jardins des environs de Paris,* **published in 1861. His book was an early survey of the way in which orangeries, conservatories, and pavillions were being used to ornament public parks in Europe.**

ABOVE **Created in 1891, The Enid A. Haupt Conservatory in the New York Botanical Gardens is the largest Victorian glasshouse in the USA. Its Palm Court, with a spectacular 27.5m (90ft) dome and dramatic reflecting pool surrounded by lush tropical plants, is home to an indoor horticultural environment that shifts from a tropical rainforest to an arid desert gallery.**

to his house at Kew – where the Royal Botanic Gardens stand today – and several other members of the nobility followed suit. King William put a stop to greenhouse building for a few years with his hefty "window tax", but was obliged to halve the tax after only three years because the glass-making industry was suffering so severely. Queen Anne then commissioned at Kensington Palace another greenhouse, in which she would stroll with her ladies in the winter and hold supper parties during the summer months.

The vogue for building greenhouses continued during the late 1700s – many of the wealthy members of the gentry in London also enjoyed estates in the country, and greenhouses became very fashionable in elite circles. Viscount Cobham, for example, had a house and gardens designed at Stowe, in Buckinghamshire, which included two greenhouses, one of which still stands today, although it is now part of the public school.

However, it remained the Dutch who led the rest of Europe in matters horticultural, and they succeeded in growing ever more exotic fruits, including pineapples – which became hugely popular – guavas, and vines.

In the USA, too, during this time, prominent families were building grand country estates with splendid grounds, complete with summerhouses and greenhouses. English styles of architecture, furniture, and greenhouse were eagerly adopted by the North Americans, and keen horticulturalists even imported plants from London.

Until the 19th century, glass production had been difficult and expensive, but in the 1830s technological advances enabled sheet glass to be mass produced. In England, this, together with the repeal of the window tax in 1851, led to a huge rise in the popularity of public and private greenhouses. Cast- and wrought-iron frames allowed new architectural styles to emerge, including curved structures and domed roofs, which let in every ray of sun.

The first great curvilinear glasshouse in England was designed at Chatsworth for the Duke of Devonshire by Joseph Paxton, who subsequently designed the Crystal Palace in London's Hyde Park. The Palm House at the Royal Botanic Gardens at Kew was probably also inspired by the Chatsworth glasshouse. Although the latter survived World War I, it was so expensive to maintain and heat that it was deliberately blown up in 1920.

ABOVE **Conservatories became fashionable additions to the country residences of the rich and aristocratic in the late 18th and early 19th centuries. This 1835 watercolour of Valentines Mansion on the outskirts of London shows an impressive example by Charles Welstead, a fellow of the Royal Horticultural Society.**

From the mid-1800s, the successes of the Industrial Revolution in England enabled many upper- and middle-class families to add domestic conservatories to their houses – designs could even be chosen and bought from catalogues. Conservatories always had glass roofs and were heated in winter by a variety of methods. Initially, they were used as reception rooms, in which exotic plants could be grown and admired. Later, intimate dinners and small parties were held in these somewhat informal domestic conservatories, which were often decorated with Indian or Oriental furniture. Ferns and potted palms became all the rage, and Victorian couples would wander through lush foliage and sit together at discreetly placed, small wrought-iron or bamboo tables.

Gradually, flowering species, such as camellias and rhododendrons, were added to the ferns, and all the plants were moved toward the outside of the room, leaving a central area for sofas and armchairs and where visitors could socialize. Conservatories became rooms in which to relax and enjoy leisure time; plants and flowers were no longer the main focus, but instead became part of the overall decoration.

In the USA, in the second half of the 1800s many public parks were created in cities, and these often contained large greenhouses and glasshouses. Philadelphia's spectacular glass palace, the Horticultural Hall, opened in 1876 as part of the city's centenary celebrations. The turn of the century saw the construction of the glasshouse in New York's Central Park and the wonderful Enid A. Haupt Conservatory at the New York Botanical Garden in the Bronx; half a dozen restorations later, this is still one of the world's finest glasshouses.

In the first half of the 20th century, two world wars, along with the world recession that resulted from the Wall Street crash in 1929, put an end to the boom in conservatories and they became luxury items once more. It was not until the 1970s that the fashion for private conservatories took hold again – a trend that has flourished ever since.

ABOVE and RIGHT By the Victorian age the conservatory was no longer the sole preserve of the social and financial elite. Above, a middle-class Victorian woman knits in the conservatory of her house, while surrounded by exotic palms and plants including Morning Glory vine. Right, a wedding takes place on the lawn in front of a "bump-out" style conservatory in north-west London in 1857

The new millennium has already provided the world with some spectacular public greenhouses, including an amazing underground one containing a fabulous tropical rainforest at the Gare de Lyon in Paris. But modern public greenhouses are no longer just for show, they are also serious scientific laboratories for the study of entire ecosystems with breeding programmes for rare and threatened species. The largest of these is the Eden Project, which is sited in an old china clay quarry in Cornwall, England. Here, complete ecosystems are housed in huge "biomes". The aim is for renewable energy to power the entire project and for all the water used to be recycled.

Nowadays, domestic conservatories are seen as extensions of the living area, and plants within them are very often peripheral. A conservatory can enhance a home in any number of ways – as a living room, a kitchen/dining room, a pool room, or an office. A conservatory does not have to be an extension on the back of a house: two separate buildings can be joined stylishly with one, or you could gain extra space and light by adding one to a flat roof. Conservatories effectively bring the garden into the house and the house into the garden and have become incredibly popular throughout Europe,

ABOVE An ultra–modern conservatory built in London in 2003 pushes glass technology to a new level, with glass walls acting as cantilevers to support a glass roof. The result is something that is nearly not a room, dissolving the distinction between indoors and outdoors.

RIGHT A glasshouse in Big Sur in California takes a contrasting approach to melding indoors and outdoors. Designed by local architect Mickey Meunnig, the project uses traditional materials to create a modern, organic architecture that harmonizes with the dramatic landscape of the area.

Australia, and North America. Adding a conservatory to your home can allow you to live more comfortably without having to move to a larger property, and this is one of the best ways to add value to your property.

Naturally, adding a conservatory to your home will present challenges of its own. Where will you site it? Which direction will it face? What is its function to be? How will you heat and ventilate it? And, of course, how much are you willing to pay for it? It is sensible to spend plenty of time thinking about your wants and needs and researching the options available before you begin. You should also check with your local planning authorities because you may need to obtain planning permission for a conservatory.

Whatever you decide – and whether you choose to use the extra space as another living room, a games room, or even an office – you will find that a conservatory has a liberating and informal atmosphere that will be completely different from that of any other room in your house – a space that you can decorate, furnish, and light in an alternative way. Perhaps best of all, a conservatory allows you to live closer to the natural world, while at the same time you remain safely in the comfort of your own home.

1

Choosing the right conservatory

Whether you buy an "off-the-peg" conservatory, choose one from a specialist supplier, or commission an architect to design a customized extension, it should be a place of inspiration, a space in which to dream. Imagine the pleasure of enjoying the last of the natural light as you read your book, tend your plants, or simply relax and look at the garden from the comfort of your own glass palace.

Once you have taken the decision to add a conservatory to your home, you will need to think carefully about how you want to use it. If your main focus is to create a space in which to grow tender or exotic plants, your conservatory will not need to be as large as if you decide to use it as another living space or a kitchen/dining room. Discuss your plans with your family – alternative ideas may be raised that you have not thought of and that will need to be considered.

Light plays an important part in all our lives, and one of the joys of conservatories is that they are light-filled spaces. However, conservatories are most often built against the house, using one or two walls, so adding such a structure can mean that you lose some light from your existing rooms. One way of dealing with this problem is to try to integrate the conservatory with the house by opening up the space to create an open-plan area. Although this will mean that you will lose some of the heat that would otherwise have been retained by the wall or walls, opening up the area will minimize the loss of natural light. Indeed, you may even gain some light, if the structure is south or west facing. (You can install a good heating system to make up for the heat loss.)

Of course, you will need to balance your requirements for light with those for space and privacy. If you want to use the conservatory as an office or studio, for example, an entirely separate room will be much more convenient than an open-plan area. Think about using glass walls or doors between the new and existing rooms, or make sure that you include windows in the adjoining wall to ensure that you maximize the amount of natural daylight in the house.

ABOVE This American "bump-out", or curved lean-to, was incorporated into the house at the time of building. It is raised to match the level of the rest of the ground floor, which is accessed by steps. Doors at the side open onto the deck at the end of the house and to steps leading down to the patio and the garden.

PREVIOUS PAGES This would have been a straightforward lean-to conservatory were it not for the addition of the dormer. This provides extra height within, while from the outside, the fanlight, finial, and cresting add elegant touches. The whole splendid structure opens onto wide steps, which lead down to the garden of this townhouse.

LEFT A conservatory can provide a marvellous way of making the most of a roof terrace – on pleasant days you can sit and eat alfresco, but you can still enjoy the view in comfort from indoors if it is too cold or wet outdoors. Plant hardy evergreens and add colour in the summer months by bringing out the flowering species that you have nurtured inside throughout the winter.

ABOVE A stunning Gothic conservatory makes a perfect addition to the side of this house, which does not benefit from much light. The style of the windows has been carefully chosen to mirror the existing ones, and the size is in good proportion to the main building. High-level ventilation ensures proper airflow through this conservatory.

Once you have settled on how the room is going to be used, give some thought to its dimensions. The furniture that you will need in your new space will have a direct bearing on its size. A family living room will need to hold armchairs, one or two sofas, a table, and possibly a television or a music centre – enough furniture, in other words, to comfortably accommodate your family and friends. A dining room will need a table and chairs and possibly a sideboard. An office may need a desk and chair, a computer and printer, shelves, and cupboard space. Try drawing up a rough plan to give yourself an idea of how large an area you will need in order to accommodate such essential furnishings.

Conservatories are extremely versatile and can add a great deal to your way of life. It is well worthwhile putting in the time to research all the alternatives. With the assistance of an architect (who will be able to help you apply for planning permission if it is needed, and will deal with relevant authorities should you live in a listed building or in a conservation area) or a specialist manufacturer, you will almost certainly find a solution that is just right for you and your particular needs.

Location

Many people have little choice as to where to site a conservatory and will have to position it at the back of the house, but if you live in a detached house you could choose to place a conservatory to one side or use it to join the house to an existing outbuilding. Where outside space is non-existent or very limited, you may be able to extend your living space with a conservatory built at first-floor level on a flat roof. On the other hand, if you have a large garden with a feature – a pond, perhaps – that is not visible from the house, why not create a separate conservatory that will enable you to enjoy a new view to the full?

The direction in which the conservatory faces will have a bearing on the amount of light and heat it receives and will affect your heating costs and the plants you can grow. Think about how you are going to use the space. A breakfast room will benefit from being east facing, for example, whereas a living room might work better facing west or south. A north-facing conservatory could be perfect for an office: you will benefit from the space but without too much summer heat. Although a south-facing conservatory may seem ideal – it will enable you to enjoy the best of the sunshine during the winter, and

ABOVE Here, location is crucial: the purpose of this conservatory is as much concerned with the view of a beautifully planted courtyard as it is about the space within. The modern wall-to-wall, floor-to-ceiling, sliding glass door creates minimal visual distraction, effectively bringing the outside – planting as well as sunshine – indoors.

the heat that will accumulate will reduce your heating bills – you will need to provide sufficient ventilation and shade to protect against the full strength of the summer sun.

A north-facing conservatory may be best for plants that thrive in cooler temperatures and are happy with some shade. It will be cooler in the summer but will need extra heating in winter. An east-facing conservatory will likewise receive little direct light during the winter. In the summer, however, it will be full of the morning sun, which is very beneficial for plant growth, and it will be protected from the worst of the strong afternoon heat. The sun could easily damage plants in a west-facing conservatory unless they are protected by blinds or receive some shade from trees in the garden, but a west-facing conservatory will be warmer overall because it will receive light all afternoon. And, of course, you will be able to enjoy watching the sun go down.

Think, too, about the shade the house will throw on your conservatory, and if you have trees or large shrubs in the garden, or in a neighbouring garden, check the shade that they throw too, as this could influence the position or shape of the conservatory you choose.

LEFT Many new conservatories are built on a dwarf wall. Although this design is fairly small, it incorporates some of the masonry that formed the original flat-roofed extension here, which lends a solid feel to the new room. A bright new sitting area has been achieved, providing easy access to the small back garden.

Historical styles

The inspiration for adding a conservatory to your house may well have sprung from your enjoyment of someone else's, but that does not mean that you want yours to be exactly the same. As you begin to look into the matter, you will find that there are many different shapes and sizes of conservatory available, as well as many different architectural styles from which to choose.

As a general rule of thumb, you should aim to match the historical style of a new conservatory with that of your house – a Victorian-style conservatory will generally look its best when added to a Victorian house, for example, while an ultra-modern structure is most suitable for a modern building. (As with everything else, there are exceptions that prove the rule, but it is always useful to have some sort of starting point.) In the end, of course, your own taste is likely to have a large influence on the style you choose, and although you may seek advice from a specialist designer – and it is often a good idea to do so – you are under no obligation to accept their recommendations . After all, you are paying for the conservatory and you are going to be living in it.

OPPOSITE This semi-circular conservatory is neatly sited between two corners of the house. Steps beside and behind it lead onto a semi-circular first-floor balcony. The roof lantern is low and rounded in order to avoid obscuring too much of the view from the two full-length windows above.

Types of conservatory

STRAIGHT-EAVE LEAN-TO

CURVED-EAVE LEAN-TO

HIP-END LEAN-TO

STRAIGHT-EAVE
DOUBLE PITCH

BULL-NOSE DOUBLE
PITCH

DOUBLE PITCH WITH
DORMER

HIP-END LEAN-TO WITH
HIP-END DORMER AND
ENTRYWAY

LEAN-TO WITH TWO
BULL NOSES

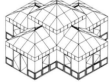

CROSS-SHAPED DOUBLE PITCH
WITH PYRAMID LANTERN

Conservatories are available in a wide
range of styles and dimensions. Choice of
shape and size will depend on how and
where the new room is to join the house
and what it is to be used for. Designs
vary from traditional styles with period
features and other embellishments to
modern, plainer constructions.

Conservatory styles tend to be named after historical periods, but manufacturers and suppliers seem to use these terms fairly loosely. If you are looking for a conservatory to match the historical style of your house, you will need to look at each individual design rather than just telling a supplier that you are looking for an Edwardian style to complement your Edwardian house, for example. You might be informed that a particular range does not include an Edwardian-style conservatory, when in fact the supplier's Regency design might be just what you are looking for. (I have recently come across a "Mediterranean"-style conservatory that looks more like a modern glass box than anything I have seen in the south of France or Spain!)

Generally speaking, the Classical style of conservatory is reminiscent of the orangeries of the past (see pages 7–9). Rectangular in shape, with columns of wood or masonry between the windows, a Classical design might have a frieze beneath the guttering, stone insets (or cast-resin stone) around the windows, or a pediment in the gable. The effect will be both solid and symmetrical.

This period house did not lend itself easily to the addition of a conservatory – the only place for it was on a rather lovely old terrace at the back, where it somewhat diminishes the look of the wing behind it. From the point of view of practicality, however, it adds a spacious dining and sitting area and gives a splendid view of the garden. In an ideal world, a stand-alone glasshouse might have been a better option here.

LEFT A lovely, wooden, triple-gabled conservatory has been placed along the length of the back of this townhouse, adding a magnificent dining and living area. The central doors open onto the patio garden, which is adorned with a variety of ornamental pots and containers. The paintwork adds colour to what was a rather severe, white rear elevation.

Georgian, Regency, and Edwardian styles all seem to be rather similar. Rectangular in shape, with tall, fairly narrow windows, they sometimes have hipped roofs (see page 21) with simple roof cresting and/or finials. The difference between these styles may be merely that of stone, brick, or wooden inserts between the windows and less (Georgian) or more (Regency and Edwardian) steeply pitched roofs.

The Victorian era was the period during which domestic conservatories became available to the middle classes, who were also beginning to take advantage of the opportunities to travel and explore more of the world than had ever before been available to them. The Victorians liked everything to be decorated, and they extended this ideal to their architecture. Victorian-style conservatories are therefore often highly ornamental in style. They tend to have rather steeply pitched roofs that are covered in ornate cresting and finials, hexagonal or octagonal bays, gables, or roof lanterns. A Victorian-style conservatory may also feature fanlights under the eaves, separated from the windows or doors beneath by a transom.

OPPOSITE An Edwardian-style conservatory has been added to the back of this house. It not only provides extra space but also links the existing house to a renovated and extended outbuilding. The difficulty with this design is that two of the house's windows, which are at a lower level than the main first-floor ones, have been partially obscured. The only way of avoiding this would have been to put on a flat roof.

OPPOSITE A thoroughly modern dining area has been added to this house at right angles to the body of the building. Access is from the kitchen, and doors on both sides of the conservatory open onto gardens. On the glazed side of the dining room, tall glass doors lead to a patio garden, while from the opposite side, which has a brick, wood, and glass construction, the doors open onto a more informal country garden for a completely different feel.

RIGHT This Bauhaus-style German conservatory is supported on poles to sit at first- and second-floor level. It provides a small, informal living space at the bottom and a balcony, accessed from the bedroom, at the top. Excellent ventilation has been provided for both areas, and the bright hues make it an even more eye-catching structure.

BELOW Here is a simple, lean-to construction that has been built along the full length of the rear of the house. It has large doors opening onto the patio, while French doors from the kitchen and sitting room give access to the new dining/living area, allowing more use to be made of the garden.

Gothic style normally refers to narrow, arched windows, often with curved glazing bars, beneath a steeply pitched roof with cresting and large finials. A Gothic-style conservatory may have one or even two dormers, and possibly decorative bargeboards as well. The word "Gothic" refers to the style of architecture that was often used in churches and religious buildings in Western Europe between the 12th and 16th centuries. It was much admired by travellers during the 19th century and championed in England by the art critic John Ruskin.

If you have a modern house and are looking for a contemporary-style conservatory to complement it, you do not have to settle for an ugly box-style structure with a polycarbonate roof. However, for this style of conservatory in particular, it is worth commissioning a good architect or finding a specialist manufacturer to help you. Modern designs are often stunning, and modern materials are being improved upon all the time.

Types of structure

As you travel around the country or look out of a train window in many places in Great Britain, you will be struck by the great number of Victorian- and Edwardian-style conservatories that have been added to suburban homes built during the second half of the 1900s. These tend to be "off-the-peg" structures bought from a good garden centre or from one of the many manufacturers of pre-fabricated conservatories. Sometimes they are in the form of a flat-pack kit, which you can put up yourself, and assembly instructions are usually accurate and helpful. The main benefits of pre-fabricated conservatories are the speed with which they can be built, and the fact that they are relatively inexpensive.

However, this type of standard structure is totally unsuitable for the type of period buildings that were constructed using the high-quality materials that were readily available at the time. Such a house requires a well-thought-out, well-built conservatory, which will be expensive. Unless you have decided upon an eye-catching modernist design, you will want your conservatory to blend in with your house and to appear to be a natural extension of it rather than an obvious add-on.

ABOVE Metal conservatories are still made by bespoke manufacturers. This hexagonal French one has a pleasing simplicity of design. The large, plain windows have simple curved glazing bars beneath the eaves and moulded designs at the base. Adjoining the original doors to the garden, the structure does not detract in any way from the form of the house.

ABOVE A most unusual Classical style double conservatory has been added here to join two buildings. One is a simple lean-to, which leads to the larger room, providing easy access between the two without the need to step outside. These two conservatories would be excellent places in which to grow plants.

Conservatories are popular throughout Europe, North America, and Australia, with each country's own architectural styles mirrored in its conservatory design. It may seem strange to think of homes in the south of France, Italy, or Australia sporting conservatories – after all, they have longer, hotter summers than those of northern Europe. However, even in such warmer climes winters can be very hard, and a conservatory can be used to house plants that need to be overwintered inside before being moved outside in the summer. A conservatory will also provide a cooler, shadier spot in which to relax when it is too hot to be out in the full sun.

Conservatories are becoming increasingly popular in urban areas and create wonderful ways of maximizing small areas. With towns and cities becoming ever more densely populated, space is often at a premium, and moving is not always feasible for any number of reasons. The location of suitable employment, proximity to the best local school, or simply the sheer cost and inconvenience of moving to a larger home all have to be taken into consideration. Rather than move, it is often a better option to simply add a conservatory and free up more space within your existing home instead.

A flat-roofed extension is an ideal site for a conservatory, as is a roof terrace. A first-floor conservatory supported on poles or columns could be a possibility. Or perhaps you have enough room to build a two-storey conservatory, with an entrance into your house from both floors and possibly even a staircase linking the two new glass rooms. Many city dwellers either have no garden at all, or merely access to a communal garden. Building a

RIGHT A modern dining room has been added to the back of this old stone house, the interior of which was quite dark. The windows of the house are relatively small and the ceilings quite low, but this lean-to has achieved a modern look, which, though it is quite different from the rest of the house in style, is complementary.

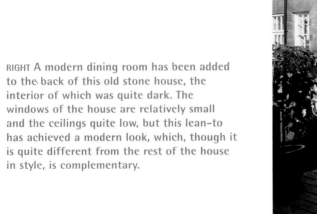

OPPOSITE The desire to use the space throughout the year informed the decision to include a fireplace in this Illinois conservatory. Using stone for the base wall and chimney helps to visually join this structure to the house and veranda, while white-painted hardwood matches the clapboard façade, making a desirable new room. High-level ventilation discreetly aids air circulation, and the ridge crest and windows, decorated only at the top, complete the bold design.

RIGHT This is an excellent example of how to make the most of a small space. The dark basement has been opened up with French doors to the garden area, and a dwarf wall above has been reinforced and tied into the walls on either side to support the conservatory, which, while narrow, is sufficiently spacious to become an informal living room. A metal tie across the front of the conservatory not only adds extra strength but also prevents accidents.

conservatory to an upper floor will enable you to feel closer to nature – and the views can be spectacular, especially at night.

It is not always easy to achieve the "natural extension" look, particularly if you have an ancient cottage located deep in the countryside, and even more difficult if you have a thatched roof. Cottages of this type sometimes sport a circular or octagonal glasshouse that somehow looks completely out of place. One solution that is occasionally used with a thatched roof is to continue the thatch and create a sunroom instead of a conservatory, but even if the roof line and pitch are followed faithfully, the glass walls beneath will look incongruous. In such a situation, it is more appropriate to keep it simple and build a small, discreet conservatory – perhaps a lean-to structure. Don't forget that it does not have to be bright white.

Conservatories can, of course, be added to a house for purely practical reasons, and not merely because an extra room is desirable. For example, I live in a converted Victorian chapel that had a separate building at the back in which the minister kept his horse and trap. During its conversion from chapel to house, it seemed sensible to join the two buildings together, which was done by putting in a lean-to conservatory that runs from what was once the back door through to the end of the stable.

ABOVE LEFT This is an interesting view of a first-floor conservatory, built on an existing flat roof. The building itself is on a hill in and commands splendid views of the surrounding Italian countryside from the windows on the upper floor. A conservatory here makes an excellent addition to a previously unused area.

LEFT This lovely double-height conservatory, a style popular in Germany, has been added to part of the back of the house, affording plenty of extra space and light. The downstairs living area is open to the apex, and French doors from the first floor bedroom open onto a decorative iron balcony enclosed within the whole.

BELOW LEFT A good deal of thought has gone into the design of this Classical-styled conservatory, which fills the space between two wings of the house. This area would always have been shaded and the addition of a lantern maximizes the amount of light that it can now receive. The conservatory provides a rather grand entryway to the rear of the house but is in keeping with the overall style.

This area now gives access to a bedroom and bathroom, houses utilities such as a washing machine and dryer, freezer, and fridge, and provides a breakfast area for guests to enjoy. It is particularly useful to us because the chapel windows are all in stained glass that one cannot see through. Now at least we are able to enjoy looking at the garden from one part of the house.

We tend to think of conservatories as being at the back of the house, but of course this does not have to be the case. It is perfectly possible to locate a conservatory at the front of the house, either running along the whole width or providing a more or less spacious porch or entryway. The Edwardians were very fond of adding glass porches, and you can still occasionally see such designs in Great Britain, especially at coastal resorts.

Glass porches are sometimes added to houses where the front door opens directly onto the sitting room. They keep a house of this type warmer and provide somewhere in which to keep coats and boots. A small, simple porch of this type looks attractive even on an old cottage. On a row of old workers' cottages, a porch, far from looking incongruous, can add extra character to a house. Keen gardeners will find enough room to grow one or two plants in such a space as well, and a porch will protect tender species from winter frosts.

RIGHT An Edwardian-style greenhouse, complete with roof lantern for extra height and light, is well suited to the style of both the house and garden here. The painted hardwood frame looks elegant, and the careful choice of silver and green foliage and white flowers is both subtle and attractive.

Materials

OPPPOSITE A good example of a Victorian-style conservatory: the roof ridge runs at 90 degrees to the main house, and there is an octagonal front section. Bricks have been selected to match those of the house, while plain, varnished hardwood has been used for the frame.

During the Industrial Revolution, new techniques for producing iron and glass were put to stunningly beautiful use in large public buildings and, later, in domestic settings. Toward the end of the 19th century, ever more ornate decoration became fashionable, and finials and fanlights, ridge crests and gables, and even details such as floor grills and brackets were made of intricate ironwork and considered highly desirable even on quite modest conservatories. Sadly, iron suffers from rusting and can be badly affected by frost, so many of the original domestic Victorian conservatories have not survived.

Today, the choice of materials to use when building a conservatory is much wider, and includes timber, harvested from sustainable forests, aluminium, and UPVC (ultraviolet-resistant polyvinyl chloride). Wood is the most traditional material and is much more in keeping with older properties than are other options, but it is relatively expensive and requires regular upkeep.

Hardwood is the best-quality material and is the natural choice of bespoke design companies. It comes from slow-growing trees, such as oak and beech, sourced from

commercial forests in Great Britain and Europe, or from tropical trees, such as mahogany and teak, from forests around the world. Unhappily, hardwoods are so sought after and so valuable that there is a thriving trade in illegal logging in many of the less-developed countries of the world, which is one of the main reasons that rainforests are disappearing at a rapid speed. Hardwood is very fine grained and so dense that it does not need to be coated with a preservative. It does not even need to be painted because it mellows naturally with age, though you can paint or stain it any colour you want.

Softwoods such as cedar and pine from North America are also very high-quality woods. European pine grows faster than the North American variety but is less strong and more prone to warping. Preservative, paint, or staining are essential for protection against the weather. Ideally softwood should be used internally rather than externally.

Aluminium is very strong, which means that much narrower glazing bars can be used. The manufacturing process allows for production of different shapes – curved roofs, for example. Because metal conducts heat very successfully, it can also feel cold, and aluminium

ABOVE **This hotel in Italy has a lovely metal-framed conservatory with doors running all along the front. These fold back to make the whole thing feel as though it is in the open. Set on a stepped hillside overlooking the sea, the conservatory provides a lovely site for the hotel's pool room.**

RIGHT Tiled and brick built, this sunroom provides a useful area between the swimming pool and the sitting room. For those who prefer not to stay in direct sunlight for too long, it affords a comfortable spot in which to relax with a drink between swims. When the pool is lit, it can be admired in comfort.

BELOW UPVC pre-fabricated conservatories are readily available from garden centres and catalogues. If you are a DIY enthusiast you will find plenty of choice in design, and those supplied by a reputable firm are usually quite straightforward to erect. The polycarbonate roof panels provide good insulation, although, unlike glass, they are not clear.

frames need to have thermal breaks built in to help prevent condensation, heat loss, and heat gain. Aluminium bars are polyester powder-coated, which makes further maintenance unnecessary. Aluminium is also considerably more ultraviolet-light resistant than plastic. One option would be to construct the conservatory walls from wood and the roof from aluminium. The narrow roof bars would maximize the available light and be maintenance free. Internally the aluminium bars could be covered with wood to match the walls.

While UPVC can look out of place on an older building, it will suit a recently built house that has windows with the same material. UPVC is not particularly strong and should be strengthened by an aluminium, or a more costly stainless-steel, core. It is popular because it is inexpensive, low-maintenance, and is easy to work with. However, the choice of colour is limited – usually white, brown, or imitation wood – and ultraviolet rays from the sun will eventually fade and degrade the plastic. Roofs made of polycarbonate sheets provide good insulation but are not clear. Glass is more expensive, but inexpensive seals around the double-glazing cavity can break down, allowing moisture to seep in and cause misting.

In recent years we have become far more aware of our environment and of the importance of energy efficiency and of using renewable resources. Great Britain lags behind Germany, the Netherlands, and Scandinavia in this regard, all of whom are extremely keen to be "green". Perhaps surprisingly, the USA is at the forefront of renewable energy technologies.

Unfortunately, most of the "off-the-peg" conservatories that are available rely heavily on the use of plastics in their construction, which in the long term is a serious problem. Plastic does not biodegrade, and there is no satisfactory way of recycling it. If it is burned, it releases noxious gases and carbon dioxide, thereby adding to the "greenhouse" effect. It cannot be buried in landfill sites, and a need for reusing second-hand PVC has yet to be found. In fact, the plastic that we use today will still be around until a safe way of recycling it has been found – and that could be hundreds, if not thousands, of years hence. If you have a concern for the environment, you should think hard before you add a plastic conservatory to your house.

ABOVE **An interesting "green" glasshouse in Germany that grew organically from a garden shed. It is used mainly for growing plants but also as a charming, private little getaway. The lichen growing on part of the roof provides extra insulation, and the tinted roof panels help protect the plants from too much direct sunshine.**

ABOVE RIGHT The steep pitch of this modern lean-to follows the line of the house roof, and the building faces south for maximum gain of solar energy. The four solar panels extend above the apex, enabling the room to receive as much light as possible.

Instead, you might consider how best to make an environmentally friendly building and perhaps find an architect or manufacturing company to help you. You could also get in touch with one of the green organizations for advice. The Centre for Alternative Technology in Machynlleth, Wales – Europe's leading eco-centre – runs courses on green building techniques, for example, and many similar organizations have sprung up worldwide. There are also numerous books about green living and building techniques that are full of interesting ideas. *The Solar Living Source Book* is a fascinating eye-opener into the world of sustainable living; packed full of tips, it also provides useful addresses and sources of further information. You might also get in touch with your local authority – advice and even financial help may be available for particular aspects of green technology.

A green conservatory might use straw-bale technology for dwarf walls, solar systems for heating, cooling, and light, and hardwood bought from a sustainably harvested forest for the frame. Glass technology is moving at a very fast pace: triple-glazing is readily available, and windows can be treated with a low-emissivity coating, which allows in solar energy but prevents heat loss. You can also use natural materials for the floor, which can be very well insulated, as well as organic paints and stains.

You may find that putting all of these ideas into practice is just too difficult – too expensive, even – though bear in mind that the initial outlay for a solar system is compensated by lower bills forever. But even if you insist only on good insulation and organic paints, you will have done something to help the planet.

Plans and reality

The plan shown above is one of many that were drawn up for a bespoke conservatory added to the turn-of-the-century, semi-detached house in West London shown opposite. Originally, the dining room had a glass roof and a solid rear wall just behind the wicker chairs that you can see here. The kitchen, which is at right angles to the table, was a separate room, accessed through a door. It had a solid roof and was dark and rather unwelcoming. Both the internal kitchen wall and the rear wall were removed to create a large, airy space, with doors opening to the patio and the garden.

The owners of the house do a considerable amount of business entertaining and so chose to move the refectory table and chairs from their existing position, as seen here, into the new part of the conservatory, which enabled the view of the garden to be enjoyed and the kitchen area to become less visible. Plenty of high-level ventilation has been included to help remove the moisture that is generated from the kitchen, which is visually divided from the conservatory both by a change of flooring and a large slab of polished-granite that functions as a work surface.

ABOVE LEFT If you are not an architect or a designer, it can be hard to look at plans or drawings and picture what they will look like in reality. Ask your designer if he/she has plans of any similar conservatories made in the past, with photographs of the finished product – this may help you to visualize your own plans more effectively.

ABOVE and OPPOSITE Exterior and interior views of the conservatory shown in the plan. Built at right angles to the house, which already had a much smaller conservatory, it has opened up a wonderfully bright space. The maple floor adds a touch of warmth. This addition has brought much needed extra light and space into the house as well as adding to its value.

2

Decorating styles

The style of your conservatory will be affected largely by its use – a living room, kitchen, dining room, home office, and bathroom will each call for its own decorative treatment. But your choice of materials and colours, particularly for flooring, will also influence the style. Even practical elements, such as heating, ventilation, and type of glass, can be chosen with style in mind to create a particular look and feel.

The Victorians' vision of a conservatory was of a place in which to grow, tend, and display exotic plants. In keeping with the decorative style of the era, all the available space was filled. Palms, ferns, and ivies were planted in large, decorative pots, climbing roses and clematis clambered up the walls, and flowering pot plants were arranged on carefully placed étagères. Paths wound their way through the foliage, and there were occasional tables and chairs around which tea could be taken or intimate supper parties held. Victorian conservatories were never sited next to the kitchen, which was seen as the servants' territory. Instead, they adjoined the drawing room or perhaps the library.

Contemporary conservatories usually serve a rather different purpose and are often built to improve and extend a kitchen/dining area. Far more attention is given to their use by people – plants are often, though by no means always, a secondary consideration.

If you are a keen gardener, you may like to consider exactly what type of plants you are planning to grow before you plan the interior of your conservatory. Avoid a carpeted or wooden floor if you are going to be doing a lot of watering – stone paving slabs or tiles

PREVIOUS PAGES An understated, elegant conservatory sitting room has been added to this house, giving views of the countryside beyond. Grey slate floor tiles are grouted in white, which picks up on the white-painted brick wall that the conservatory abuts. A vine, laden with black grapes, looks magnificent.

ABOVE Bookshelves and plenty of cupboard space have been built in against one of the two solid walls in this conservatory-cum-study. Usually used for doing homework, reading the newspaper, and writing letters, the table is easily large enough to seat six for breakfast or lunch. Flowering shrubs in decorative pots add colour to the area, as do the books.

ABOVE RIGHT **In this London flat, space is at an absolute premium. The owners have cleverly knocked their kitchen through and built a simple, lean-to conservatory that adjoins the boundary wall. This has afforded them enough extra space to make a glazed dining area in what had been a difficult, underused patio.**

would be more suitable. If you need to have high humidity in the conservatory, you will have to make sure that any furniture will not be damaged by it – rattan and wicker tend to degrade far less quickly than ordinary upholstered furniture. Where are you going to place your plants? Will you need trellises or pillars for climbers? If you have a dwarf wall, will the sill be deep enough to hold pots, and from what are you going to hang baskets? Glazing bars are not sufficiently strong for this, but you can use a tie bar or an internal beam, if there is one. If you are tending a lot of plants, make sure a tap is fitted. Really serious gardeners will want to have beds constructed – plants can really thrive when they have enough space, so either leave an area of the floor without concrete or construct a raised bed. Sophisticated, computer-controlled watering systems are available, but a hosepipe is difficult to disguise, unless the plants are growing in beds.

Even if you want to use the new room primarily as a living space, plants will grow perfectly well in decorative pots or tubs, and you can place these wherever you wish, moving some of them onto the patio or into the garden during the summer months.

RIGHT The lean-to dining area that has been added here has been seamlessly joined to the kitchen. The use of the same flooring links the two areas together visually, as does the paintwork. From a practical point of view, the person preparing and cooking meals can talk to friends sitting at the table or help children with homework.

Different rooms

OPPOSITE This superb Victorian glasshouse, made of curved metal and wood, provides a splendid area in which to relax in this historic house. The ornate décor – large plants in elaborate containers, upholstered chairs, a large mirror, and a traditional ceiling fan – suits the opulence of this unusual conservatory perfectly.

Generally speaking, today's conservatories are more often concerned with people than plants. Although a great many are used as dining areas and sitting rooms, they are also well suited to use as kitchens, offices, and even luxurious spa bathrooms. Even if you are able to claw only a little extra depth into a room, it can be put to much better use than a patio of the same size, which can often be very awkward.

A common choice is to use a conservatory as a living room, whether this is a formal sitting room or an informal family room. For many families with children, having a second living area makes an enormous difference to life, for example when guests have been invited for a meal only for the hosts to discover at the last minute that the living room is full of toys. The British tend to use conservatories as secondary, informal living rooms, because the main room of the house is generally the largest and most suitable for this purpose. This is not necessarily the case in other countries, where the conservatory or sunroom might be built at the same time as the house. Particularly if there is a superb view to be admired, this could well be the area most suitable to use as the sitting room.

ABOVE Designed as a small, bright playroom, this conservatory has plenty of shelf space, where toys can be put away at the end of the day. Doors lead out to an enclosed patio garden, allowing the children to play both indoors and out, while remaining within sight of their parents.

LEFT A rather stylish modern conservatory sitting room was added here to enable the owners to enjoy good views of their north-facing garden. No blinds or curtains are needed, because the room never gets too hot, yet plants receive enough light to prosper.

OPPOSITE This modern German conservatory makes good use of the hillside upon which the house is built. The striking pale wood is carried through from the rest of the ground floor, as is the tiled floor. Steps lead down to an informal sitting room that is full of light, and there are plants at all levels. Ceiling and wall blinds provide shade for people and plants.

RIGHT A country conservatory to die for. Foliage and flowers abound in this peaceful, rustic dining room. The furniture picks up the colour of the brick wall, while the painted wood suits the dark green foliage. With all the doors open, the owners can enjoy the feeling of being in the garden from inside.

BELOW Part of the patio area of this ground-floor apartment has been transformed into a bright and sunny conservatory dining room. The white walls and chairs are offset by the warmth of the wooden table and flooring, and the prettily planted patio area outside is still large enough to accommodate garden furniture and a barbecue during the summer months. Clematis climbing the white-painted trellis completes the effect.

If your sitting room is smaller than you would like or too dark for your taste, you might decide to enlarge and brighten it up by adding a conservatory at one end. In an extension of this sort you can choose which end to gravitate toward depending on the weather, the time of day, or even simply your mood. In such a situation, it is usually best to run the same flooring throughout – you can break up the expanse with rugs if you wish – and to choose furniture in the same style as that of the rest of the room. If you choose to carpet the whole area, bear in mind that you will need to use the door to the garden judiciously to avoid mud being trampled directly into your sitting room.

Another option is to use the conservatory as a kitchen and/or dining room. A very well-designed and easy-to-use kitchen can be created in a surprisingly small space – it can be advantageous to be within easy reach of every item that you need. And even the smallest of conservatories can provide you with a more spacious area in which to eat and socialize. If you choose to enlarge and extend your existing kitchen it is best to use the same flooring throughout for continuity. However, perhaps you have included a new dining area in your plans, in which case you can make a visual break between the two areas by using two different types of floor – tiles or linoleum in the kitchen and wood in the dining room, for example. You could have a breakfast bar built to divide the two areas; this would function in the same way as a hatch between the kitchen and the dining room, and children could use the breakfast bar to sit at and do their homework while supper is being prepared.

LEFT A grand piano takes up a surprisingly large amount of space that may not be spare, and it can be wearing for the other members of the family if they need to sit in the same room as someone practising. This modern conservatory is used as a music room, but it also has a table and chairs that can be enjoyed even when the instrument is not in use.

LEFT A growing number of people work from home these days, but not everyone has a room available for an office. One alternative is to add a conservatory, as this designer has done. The light is a bonus, particularly for those who are creative – such airy conservatories are inspiring places.

The growth of personal computers and the Internet has transformed the working lives of many of us, and now more and more people can work from home. However, a home office takes space, and very often there is no spare room available. This is where a conservatory might be exactly what you need. You could either make your conservatory into a new room, freeing up an existing one to become your office, or turn the new conservatory into your workspace. You will be able to shut the office door at the end of the working day and leave it all firmly behind you, and your new conservatory office will look and feel so different from your other rooms that when you leave it to return to the rest of the house, you will genuinely feel that you have gone somewhere else.

If the conservatory is east or north facing, you will benefit from extra light, particularly in summer, without suffering from too much direct sunshine. You might not need to invest in blinds for shade at all, though you may need double- or triple-glazing and heating. If the room is to be south or west facing, you will need good ventilation, and probably a ceiling fan, as well as blinds to give yourself some protection from the sun.

ABOVE The large, ornate conservatory shown here was constructed to provide an indoor, heated swimming pool for a new hotel in France. The pool area is shaded by external blinds, while most of the loungers are in sunlight. Sufficient room has been left around the pool for people to move about easily, and the urns on either side of the steps leading into the pool provide a nice finishing touch.

ABOVE This beautiful spa bathroom gives a great view of the garden – even in winter it is a peaceful sight. Blinds have been installed to ensure total privacy – and snugness, if that is what your mood requires. There is plenty of space around the bath for setting down a book and glass of wine.

ABOVE RIGHT This is a very glamorous, Californian-style swimming pool, with a separate whirlpool in the foreground for those who prefer not to swim but enjoy the therapeutic benefits of water jets. Decking has been used instead of tiles, but it is hard wearing and will not be damaged by becoming wet. The high humidity suits many species of tropical plants.

Turning the conservatory into a music room is another possibility, particularly if you can place it against two solid walls to afford the rest of the house some protection against sound (don't forget to be sensitive to your neighbours, too). If you have a good instrument, it is a sensible idea to install blinds, as direct sunlight can bleach. Wood is also vulnerable to humidity, so make sure that you have sufficient ventilation.

Installing a spa bathroom is a real treat, but think how fabulous it would be to put one into a conservatory. You may be fortunate enough to have an area that is not overlooked, but if there are issues of privacy, you can install judiciously placed blinds or curtains. Imagine lying in the bath on a bright, sunny morning, feeling glad to be alive as you look out at the garden and watch the birds. At night you might want to relax with a glass of wine, your favourite music, and scented candles as you gaze up at the night sky glittering with stars – heavenly! In the summer you could open up the doors to feel the warm breeze on your skin, and in winter, if there was snow on the ground, you could admire its cold beauty while lying in gorgeously warm water.

LEFT Another large and beautiful conservatory has been constructed for a hotel swimming pool. Often such amenities are housed in utilitarian basement areas, but if there is enough room to build one like this, it adds a real sense of luxury. A raised seating area enables guests with children to sit and enjoy a drink while keeping an eye on the offspring.

LEFT A lovely room for people and plants, this double-height conservatory is joined to the upper floor by an attractive metal spiral staircase. The dining/sitting room below benefits from the full height of the structure, allowing a full-sized palm tree room to grow, and metal steps lead up to the doors opening onto the garden.

OPPOSITE A charming Gothic garden room conservatory with cane chairs that will not be damaged by over-zealous watering and a superb view across the valley. It is absolutely dripping with plants, some at floor level and some placed on the extra-wide windowsills. The stone floor, which looks good against the terrace outside, is partially covered by a Moroccan rug, which adds warmth of colour.

LEFT In this is a conservatory plants come first. Pots and planters are placed at different levels throughout, and the whole area is a mass of flowers and foliage. This must be the gardener's secret hideaway – there is just enough room to fit in a comfortable rattan steamer chair.

RIGHT A lovely informal sitting room has been added here, with the side of the house opened to it to eye-catching effect. The handmade terracotta tiles, with their non-uniform colours, complement both the original beams and the painted frame harmoniously. During winter, rugs are placed on the tiled floor to give more warmth to the look.

Flooring

OPPOSITE In this formal garden room, where plants take precedence, the cool hues extend to the York stone floor. These stone slabs cannot come to any harm from inadvertent splashes from the watering can. The only notes of colour are derived from the variegated leaves of the plants, and all the flowers are white except for a decorative pot of golden chrysanthemums on a central table.

To an extent, the flooring you choose for your conservatory will depend on the use you are going to make of the space. If it is going to be an extension of an existing room, it will probably be best to use the same flooring throughout, though you may want to introduce a visual break by using a different material to mark the end of the kitchen and the start of the dining room, for instance.

Your choice will also be influenced by the materials from which the conservatory is made. For example, if it is constructed of unpainted hardwood, you might want to go for either a wooden floor or terracotta tiles that are roughly the same shade as the wooden frame; old floor bricks can look wonderful too. However, if the frame is painted, you might prefer ceramic tiles of a complementary hue or in pale limestone with coloured inserts.

The floor should be hard-wearing and easy to maintain, and should not be vulnerable to damage from damp or heat. Unless the room is to be an extension of your sitting room, it is best to avoid wool carpeting: strong sunlight has a bleaching effect, and if people are moving in and out of the garden the carpet, inevitably will become marked.

Floor tiles come in many shapes, sizes, and materials. They can be patterned or plain, with a smooth or textured finish, and may be quarry tiles, terra cotta, ceramic, slate, or marble. All of these are available in a variety of shades. Stone floors have a look of traditional elegance. Limestone or sandstone (of which York stone is the best known) look very good, especially if the conservatory gives onto a stone patio, which will meld the two areas together visually. Properly finished, concrete slabs can also look very effective and are less expensive – a bonus if you have a large area to cover.

Wooden flooring is easy on the eye, but take advice on the best type to use. Parquet may suffer from movement and warping, and boards can separate and crack if they are not properly finished and carefully laid. Bamboo flooring has the same feeling of warmth and natural beauty but is more stable than wood and is treated to make it water resistant.

There are also less expensive options: some lovely, solid-colour linoleum is available these days, and vinyl comes in all sorts of designs and hues. You could also consider sea-grass or sisal matting, both of which are tough and reasonably easy to maintain.

ABOVE The large sitting room shown here was designed to be as light and bright as possible. The pale furniture corresponds with the neutral sisal carpeting that extends throughout. This room makes the most of the uninterrupted, 180-degree view, while pastel blinds add warmth and colour when the sun shines through them.

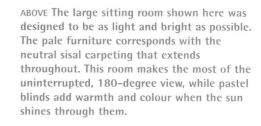

LEFT A sunny conservatory furnished in minimalist style enables the owners to sit and enjoy the plants and the view. The space has been painted white throughout, and trellis panels have been fitted against one wall with a circular "porthole" in the middle of each, providing a view of flowering shrubs that have been strategically placed to the exterior. The black-and-white tiled floor adds to the crisp, clean look.

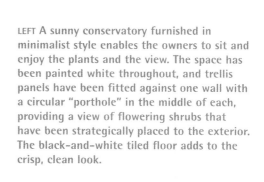

OPPOSITE This formal conservatory fills the space between two buildings. The sitting area that has been formed here has doors at the end leading to the garden. Wooden flooring has been used throughout with no change of level, though the paler wood of the new floor provides a slight visual break.

Paint colours

When you are extending an existing room into a conservatory, it is advisable to retain one colour scheme throughout. This will lead the eye all the way through without a visual break and properly integrate the two areas. You may notice, however, that the addition of a conservatory will make the original room darker than before. To counteract this, you could try painting the latter a lighter shade of the same colour.

As the interior of a conservatory is visible from outside, many people choose to use the same colour both externally and internally, although a complementary shade is equally appropriate. If your conservatory has a metal or UPVC frame, your choice will be limited to white or various shades of brown, but timber framing can be painted or stained any shade you like. There are several manufacturers of environmentally friendly paints, both oil based and water based, that are suitable for both interior and exterior use. No matter what type of paint you choose, it will need refurbishing at intervals of between three and five years. Wood that has been stained or varnished rather than painted will likewise need regular maintenance.

LEFT The soft, pale green of the woodwork and floor of this conservatory looks lovely in conjunction with the garden outside, and the blues of the furniture and upholstery mimic the colour of the sky. Together these hues achieve a charming, country-cottage effect in this comfortable sitting-and-dining area.

BELOW LEFT This small conservatory benefits from a lantern. Placed between buildings, the roof and lantern are painted white, which, together with the white flooring, makes the most of the light entering from above. The blue woodwork of the walls is a continuation of the interior room.

Most people opt for pastel or neutral hues that can be brightened with furniture and accessories. The various shades of green and blue can also be used to good effect: greens complement the foliage in the garden and blues, the sky. Yellows can look fabulous at the height of summer, but somehow seem inappropriate in northern climes in mid-winter. Other colours to consider are the earth tones – beige and buff, ochre and terra cotta. Generally, bold colours are better seen in strong sunlight, so if you live in a cooler climate, it may be best to use such shades sparingly, perhaps as accents against a more neutral background. (There are, of course, no hard-and-fast rules, and there are many lovely conservatories that make use of very vivid colours successfully.)

The function of your conservatory will also have a bearing on the colour you paint it. An office space will probably suit a neutral shade, whereas a children's playroom would look much jollier with at least some vivid colours in it. It is worth taking a good look at a variety of colour schemes before you come to your decision, though if everything goes wrong, all is not lost – you can always repaint.

RIGHT **The radiators that sit beneath the windowsill in this classically styled sitting area run the length of the room, providing plenty of heat even on chilly days. Painted white to match the window frames, they also complement the white wicker furniture.**

Heating

OPPOSITE **This lovely American conservatory has been specifically designed for use as an all-year-round sitting room with a traditional stone fireplace as its focal point. The stone floor and chimney, together with wicker and wood furniture, lend a touch of warmth to the white-painted frame.**

There are various options when it comes to heating your conservatory, but once again, you will need to think about how you are going to use the space. If plants are more important than people, determine which kinds you want to grow, and what minimum and maximum temperatures they will require. If creating space for people is your priority, consider whether the conservatory will be used only during the daytime, or whether you will also want to occcupy it during the evenings.

Underfloor heating is expensive to install, though reasonably efficient to run, and the heat produced is very comfortable for both people and plants. It has the added benefit of not taking up any floor space with radiators or other fixtures. Hot-water pipes or electric cables can be set in the screed beneath floor tiles or slabs, or installed around the edge and covered by a decorative grille.

Alternatively, you could extend your existing central heating system. However, it is not always possible to find space for radiators, and they do tend to dry the air – not helpful to plants, which may need extra humidity. Ensure that radiators are on their own thermostatically controlled circuit to enable you to fix the heat so that it never drops below your minimum temperature, even if the heating in the rest of the house is turned off completely. You can disguise radiators by boxing them in behind a decorative screen, which could give you windowsills wide enough to accommodate plant pots. Portable fires and radiators that run on oil, gas, or electricity are other options, but they take up space and are quite expensive to run.

If you know that your conservatory will be used constantly, you might consider having a fireplace built or putting in a wood-burning or multi-fuel stove, providing that the new area is sufficiently spacious. This is an effective form of heating but will have to be decided upon right at the start because a chimney or flue will have to be installed and air bricks or a ventilation grille put in to ensure a permanent flow of fresh air to the room. A fireplace tends to be the focal point of a room, and a wood fire is a very attractive sight, but it will take up a certain amount of space because you will need to house containers for logs and fire tools as well as a hearth.

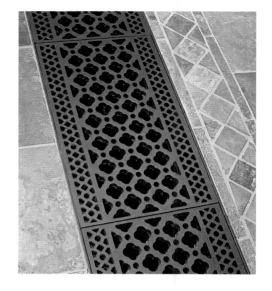

ABOVE An example of a decorative cast-iron heating grille, of which there are many different designs. They are attractive in their own right and can be customized to fit in with your colour scheme, but they should be galvanized to prevent rusting if they are likely to receive frequent watering.

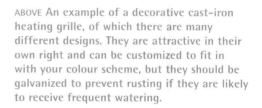

LEFT The heating system here is an extension of the system within the house. Radiators have been installed in the bay and disguised as a windowsill that is wide enough to hold large pots of plants with ease. The radiators are boxed in, leaving a fretwork fascia for heat dissemination. The paintwork matches the interior glazing bars.

OPPOSITE This conservatory has been designed specially to incorporate a full-height wood-burning stove, which has been carefully positioned to throw heat into as much of the conservatory as possible. The beauty of a stove such as this is that heat comes not only from the fire itself but also from the entire surface of the metal flue.

ABOVE High-level ventilation is an effective method of keeping the air circulating around your conservatory, particularly when there is low-level ventilation from open windows as well. These roof vents can be operated manually, at the touch of a button, or they can be connected to a temperature sensor that will control them automatically.

Ventilation

All rooms need ventilation, and conservatories need more than most in order to cool the area in summer and to prevent condensation – something that needs to be considered at the design stage. Of course, you will be able to open the doors and some of the windows, but you will need some form of permanent ventilation as well.

Hot air rises, and when it meets a cold surface, moisture in it will form condensation. Even if your conservatory is warm and dry, it is likely to produce condensation, particularly in the early days – moisture within the structure itself can take up to a year to dry out completely. High-level roof vents and trickle vents – obligatory on new windows – can help air circulate properly, and some manufacturers can provide an opening ridge to the roof. Roof vents can be operated manually, by using a pole, and automated systems are also available. A recent innovation is the solar vent, which is fitted into the roof. Ensure that your roof vents are fitted carefully to avoid any leaks.

Extractor fans can also help, but they often become noisy with age. Ceiling fans can look lovely and make little noise, though they will not solve condensation problems.

ABOVE Ceiling fans can be decorative and not merely practical. This one looks like an old, traditional hand-held fan. However, it is not the only form of ventilation in this conservatory: there are roof vents as well as doors and windows that open. With a fireplace in the room, good ventilation is essential.

OPPOSITE This modern Gothic-style conservatory is both narrow and high. Vents on either side of the roof apex help to keep the space cool during the summer and prevent condensation build-up during the winter. Too high to be easily operated by hand, the vents are electric and can be closed and opened at the flick of a switch.

Glass

As your conservatory will contain more glass than any other material, it is worth buying the best that you can afford. Building regulations will probably state that you use toughened or laminated glass, particularly at a low level and in the roof, but its use is in any case essential for safety reasons if you are planning a children's playroom, for example.

Laminated glass absorbs most of the ultraviolet rays that cause fabrics to fade and wood to bleach, and both toughened and laminated glass are very hard to break. They will almost certainly be "Low-E" (low-emission) glass, which increases insulation by about one third. Glass can be coated with various films, such as anti-sun and self-cleaning coats.

You should think about double- or even triple-glazing, or consider "Pilkington K", which is a specialist glass that has an energy-saving coating and is said to make double-glazing as effective as triple-glazing.

Finally, you could make use of decorative glass – either patterned or etched, or even stained glass. The last can be obtained from various suppliers, or you might want to incorporate original pieces into your design.

ABOVE The owners of this spacious, wood-framed conservatory have made an interesting design choice in their addition of stained-glass borders to otherwise plain glass windows and doors. The yellow panes look spectacular with the sun shining through, and the single, blue-patterned panes in the top corners of each window pick up the blue sky.

RIGHT This unusual, original cast-iron glasshouse has been made even more decorative by the use of splendid stained-glass inserts. This is a conservatory for plants, but as the stained glass is judiciously placed at the top of the walls, the plants within can still be seen to their best advantage.

BELOW Beautiful, old stained glass has been used in the doors and windows of this metal-framed conservatory, and when the sun shines through it, the effect is glorious. Most modern conservatories use plain, or sometimes frosted, glass, but there is no reason why you cannot add a touch of colour here and there.

3

Using plants

Perhaps you have always dreamed of having a place in the country where you can plant an orchard? Of course, a conservatory cannot make your dream come true, but it can help. Plant a grapevine, or a peach or nectarine, either in a bed left in the floor or in a large container, and within just a few years you will be able to walk into your conservatory in the morning and pick fresh fruit for your breakfast.

By now you will have decided on the function that your new conservatory will serve, and you will be giving some thought to the types of plants you would like to grow in it. Before you buy any plants, it is important to bear in mind the aspect of the room and the minimum temperature that you will be able to maintain there during the winter months.

In these times of easy, inexpensive, rapid travel, many of us have been smitten by plant specimens that we have seen growing in foreign climes – that mimosa in Provence, the passionflower in Costa Rica, the datura in Thailand. We all yearn to grow something special, but there is so much from which to choose – plants are available from every climate throughout the world, from tropical rainforest to mountainous areas, but sadly it is impossible to grow them all.

The plants you choose should enhance your whole experience of being in your new environment. Because a conservatory affords such a great opportunity to create a wonderful, plant-filled space, it would be a shame to squander it by placing a few, haphazardly chosen specimens at random. Given some careful thought, the plants can be as effective as your chosen colour scheme and furniture. You have probably spent time in someone else's conservatory where the planting does not do the room justice. Perhaps there were a couple of African violets, some Busy Lizzies, and a Christmas cactus

PREVIOUS PAGES The Victorian floor tiles in this pretty little conservatory look very pleasing with the reclaimed bricks that form the raised bed, and the fuschias that hang down the side soften the effect even further. The *Justicia rizzinii* is clearly well established and flourishing – its somewhat untidy habit suits this relaxed-looking space.

BELOW The gorgeous grapevine takes centre stage in this lovely, stone-floored conservatory, and clever underplanting disguises the hole in the flooring where the vine is placed. Pelargoniums grow in simple terracotta pots for added colour, and metal wall baskets and the decorative metal planter add interest to this simple room.

ABOVE RIGHT This conservatory has been carefully planned for gardening while leaving enough room for a table and chairs. Deep shelves accommodate numerous pot plants, and low-growing plants have formed a mat in a narrow bed in the floor. Honeysuckle and other climbers are trained up and across at the far end of the conservatory.

alongside some straggly herbs. A little forward planning will help you to avoid this unharmonious look. Unless friends and family know exactly what you want, it can be awkward when they offer you gifts of plants, but there will be other windowsills and sheltered spots in your home where you can place and enjoy these gifts without allowing them to clutter up the display in your conservatory.

Give some thought not only to the size of plants that you intend to grow, but also to the containers in which you will plant them. These are available in all shapes and sizes, and in many different materials. You may want to use simpler pots at ground level, keeping more decorative ones nearer eye level, where they can be seen and admired.

Do you intend to try for blooms all year round, or are you content with foliage and non-flowering plants, which can always be brightened up with bulbs, such as hyacinth and crocus or brilliant amaryllis? Orchids have become widely available and very sought after in recent times, and can they flower profusely if you are lucky with them. It is all a matter of personal taste, and it is both creative and exciting to design a planting scheme yourself.

How to use plants

You may already have a very firm idea of how you are going to plant up your conservatory. Serious gardeners will have designed the whole space around the plants they have in mind, leaving beds in the floor, building raised beds, and placing poles or columns for plants to twine themselves up. However, many of us are not quite that organized, and begin to think about planting fairly late on in the proceedings.

Talk to green-fingered friends, and buy gardening magazines and books about conservatory plants or borrow them from the library. Visit good nursery gardens to see what they have to offer and to ask advice of the knowledgeable people working there. Take your time about this. If the lack of a design bothers you, put in one or two features that you know you would like to have, such as a herb garden or a lemon tree, and work around them. At least you will have something growing and plants to look at from the beginning.

You could, perhaps, decide to make a feature of one type of plant – bougainvillea, for example. You will want to place other plants around it, so you will have to consider not only the bougainvillea itself – the fact that it will be a showy but untidy creature, its potential height, its colour, and its lack of fragrance – but also the colour, height, fragrance, and habit of everything you put around and beside it. You may want to pick plants to complement the colour of your conservatory. This can be achieved by using similar shades – white flowers and silver and green foliage for a green-and-white room, say. Alternatively, you could opt for a vivid, contrasting colour and choose plants with dark red or orangey-yellow blooms.

Another idea would be to concentrate on growing a collection of plants, such as cacti or succulents. In this scenario, you could group them all in containers, or possibly in a raised central bed. Is your conservatory suitable for hanging baskets, and will you place your plants at different levels or all on the floor? Perhaps you would like to locate all your plants in one corner of the room. The possibilities are endless.

You will also need to give some thought to the type of plant containers or pots you would like to have, and here again, there is a very wide choice. Citrus trees are traditionally planted in square, wooden "Versailles" tubs, which can either be painted or

BELOW LEFT A variety of terracotta pots and stands, both plain and decorated, planted up with a variety of primulas, spring bulbs, pelargoniums, and variegated ivy. When the bulbs have finished flowering they can be removed and stored for use the following year, and the pots can be replanted.

BELOW A lead planter such as this looks very stylish, and yet it does not detract from the terracotta pots at all. This evergreen box plant has small, dense leaves and likes sun or light shade. Trim it in the late summer, and keep it in shape by snipping off any over-enthusiastic growth.

RIGHT Raised beds have been built along the whole of one side of this conservatory despite the change of level, giving both the grapevine and the palm plenty of space to grow and prosper. The bright blooms beneath provide added interest to the eye, with some colour among the greenery.

left plain. Use a liner unless the wood is a hardwood such as iroko, teak, or oak, which will not need lining but which should be treated with Danish oil or teak oil. Terracotta pots are attractive, available in every size imaginable, and can be glazed or unglazed, and plain or decorated. There are also many beautiful ceramic pots to be found, in all styles and shades. Lead or stone tubs, too, can be very elegant, or you could opt for a more rustic look with wicker pot holders and baskets.

Don't forget that the types of plants you grow will depend to a large extent on the temperature at which the conservatory is kept, and the amount of sunlight it receives. If you can be certain that the temperature will never fall below 10°C (50°F) at night, and will rise to 18–20°C (64–68°F) during the day, plants from warm temperate and cool subtropical zones will thrive. Tropical plants will need both daytime and night-time temperatures rather higher than this, and will need to be kept humid. If you have a north-facing conservatory that receives little direct sunshine, take advice as to what will grow best – ferns would be ideal.

Mixed planting

Although the majority of conservatories are built primarily as extra rooms, most people like to grow something in them– a conservatory without plants is like a bookcase with no books – and many of us would love to enjoy a gorgeous show of flowers all year round.

If you do not want to have a room overpowered by a large, dramatic foliage plant, you may prefer a mixture of smaller flowering plants interspersed with small foliage plants to provide a constant green background. As the flowers come to an end, you can replace them with plants that are just coming into bloom. Try to make sure that the species you buy will be happy in the conditions in which they are going to live: a north-facing conservatory will require different types of plant to a west-facing one, for example.

Mixed planting in a conservatory is what we all do in our gardens but on a smaller scale. If you are clever, you can have something interesting to look at all the time – flowering and foliage plants, climbers and trailing plants. A wonderful display of spring bulbs can provide a real morale boost when winter seems to have been going on too long, but when the flowers have died down there is nothing much left to look at.

Take advice from an expert, or work out a plan for yourself. Choose one or two plants just for their foliage – perhaps ivies, ferns, or a palm. Make sure that you include species that come into flower during different seasons. You can grow annual climbers, such as the cup-and-saucer vine, *Cobaea scandens*, or morning glory, *Ipomoea* sp., which loses its leaves in winter. *Hardenbergia violacea* flowers in winter and spring, as does winter-flowering jasmine, which has the added bonus of a lovely scent. Bougainvillea can bloom throughout the year, and some robust hybrid citrus trees will also produce flowers all year round, some of which will set and become fruit. You will probably need to place a few non-deciduous plants or trailers in front of your climbers to disguise their woody stems. Cyclamen will flower for three or four months during winter, while *Streptocarpus* sp., fuchsias, and geraniums may produce blooms for months during the spring, summer, and autumn.

Smaller flowering plants can always be moved out into the garden once their season is over and replaced with specimens that are just coming into bloom. You might think of

BELOW The owner of this conservatory has successfully achieved a rather lush, exotic-looking display of plants, from ferns at floor level to Chilean bellflowers climbing up the walls, and a splendid focalpoint azalea. The real star, though, is the orange tree.

ABOVE Spring flowers make a splendid display in these pots, and the white tulips look particularly good against the green foliage. The mass of blooms on the azalea are put to good effect high up at the back of the display, with vivid blue grape hyacinths tucked in beneath them.

ABOVE RIGHT Here, a small corner in the conservatory contains a profusion of mixed plants, including climbers and trailers. The stone head looks out from behind trailing fuchsias and the tall *Campanula pyramidalis*. An oleander, *Nerium oleander*, is growing on the left-hand side, and there is a mass of *Hydrangea macrophylla* in the foreground.

keeping a few cacti – they are easy to maintain and many have interesting, architectural shapes. Cacti also produce flowers, which lend an air of exoticism.

If you want to grow many different plants in your conservatory, you will have to be prepared to work fairly hard at it. Each one will have different requirements regarding watering, feeding, cutting back, and so forth. Many people start out with a broad range of plants in their conservatory and over time become particularly interested in just one or two species, which gradually supersede everything else.

Smaller plants will be best appreciated if they are raised off the floor, which means using either an étagère or a combination of pots on plant stands, jardinières, small tables, or trolleys. The last could be hidden to some extent with trailing plants, whereas you could make decorative plant stands part of the whole display by choosing ones that complement the overall style of the room. If you have one or two pots containing taller plants such as amaryllis, try underplanting them with something small and low growing, such as a viola, or a foliage plant, for example pilea.

Climbers

ABOVE Although many climbers can be grown successfully in a pot, a small raised bed will provide plenty of growing room for them to reach their full potential. This spectacular jasmine has stunning, white, fragrant blooms.

ABOVE RIGHT Vines grow well in pots, but a full-size example grown in the ground will take up a great deal of space. However, one plant can live for thirty or more years and could provide you with vast quantities of fruit.

OPPOSITE All the climbers here are using trellis for support, though philodendrons will climb a moss pole too. They like shade, warmth, and humidity, and their glossy leaves need to be wiped regularly to look their best.

Grown up one or more of the walls or trained across part of the roof to form a leafy, shaded area beneath which to sit, climbing plants can make a big visual impact in a conservatory, and underplanting them will solve the problem of untidy-looking stems.

Most climbers need a little help, which you can provide easily in various ways. You can put in posts or pillars, or fix trellises, which can be painted the same colour as the wall if you want to disguise it, or made a feature by being painted in a quite different shade. You could also stretch horizontal lengths of plastic-coated wire up the wall and across the ceiling. Special fixings are available for attaching wires to aluminium glazing bars.

If possible, grow several different climbers so that you have a show of gorgeous flowers and/or gorgeous scents at different times of year. *Jasminum polyanthum* is a lovely climber with fragrant flowers that open in the winter or early spring and fill the room with fragrance at a time of year when it is particularly welcome. Passion flowers will establish themselves within a season or two and are good at climbing. The flowers look so exotic that it's easy to forget how handsome the fruits are, too.

Bougainvillea can be grown very successfully, although it needs a lot of space. Clematis and honeysuckle can also thrive, as will the trumpet vine, *Campsis radicans*, and morning glory, *Ipomoea* sp., though some species are poisonous. Morning glory can be grown from seed annually and has flower colours ranging from dark blue to white or pink. If given supports up which to climb, some varieties will grow as tall as 5m (16½ ft). The sweet-smelling blooms of *I. alba*, the moonflower, open in the evening and are over by mid-morning. This variety is grown as a perennial and needs cutting back in spring.

Mandevilla is another climber that is reasonably easy to grow. It has large flowers, up to 10cm (4in) wide, even on young plants, and shiny green leaves. *M.* x *amabilis* 'Alice du

ABOVE This wonderful-looking vine is covered with bunches of grapes. Both wine-producing and dessert-grape vines are available, but it takes so many grapes to make wine that it is probably sensible to opt for either vinous, sweetwater, or Muscat dessert grapes. Of these, the Muscat has the best taste.

RIGHT Roses are among the climbers clambering up the walls and around the lantern of this conservatory. Contact a specialist rose nursery for advice on what to buy. Roses need plenty of sunshine and water except during the winter rest period. They also need liquid fertilizer while in growth.

Pont' has pink flowers; *M. boliviensis* has beautiful white flowers with yellow throats. Like *Ipomoea*, they need supports up which to twine and should be pruned in late winter.

Clerodendrum thomsoniae, the bleeding heart vine, is a fabulous, showy, evergreen climber from West Africa and will grow to 3m (10ft) in height. Its scarlet flowers surrounded by white bracts look startling against a background of pointed green leaves. It likes humidity and needs frequent watering from spring until autumn. Leave it for a few weeks without watering during winter and tidy or prune it back after flowering.

Gloriosa superba 'Rothschildiana' is a tropical climbing lily from Africa and Asia with flowers made of six twirly red and yellow petals with projecting yellow stamens. The tubers, which can cause skin irritation, should be planted in spring and watered in. After this, only water again when the top third of the compost has dried out– overwatering is the quickest way of killing the lily. Continue to water carefully until the plant has died back after flowering, then store the tubers in a warm place over winter.

While considering all these exotic-looking climbers, however, don't forget the rose. There are some lovely examples, and a specialist nursery will give you advice on the best ones to choose. Make sure you go for a fragrant variety – many modern roses have no smell. 'Maréchal Niel' is a popular choice: its creamy yellow flowers have a lovely scent. 'Gloire de Dijon' is another old and fragrant rose worth considering.

LEFT This is truly a gardener's conservatory, where plants come first. The grapevine and the *Plumbago* climb up and over, while other, smaller plants – *Abutilon*, pelargoniums, and fuchsias – provide colourful splashes at different levels. An armchair enables the gardener to sit and enjoy the room.

LEFT The passionflower is one of the most extraordinary flowers, and there are so many wonderful varieties available these days that you can grow them whether your conservatory is virtually unheated or kept tropically warm. Some have edible fruit, and others have fragrant flowers, but all the larger types need regular pruning.

BELOW *Campsis*, or trumpet vine, is a very vigorous plant and it is best to grow it in a large pot to prevent it from growing bigger than you want. It is also absolutely stunning, and its racemes of trumpet-shaped flowers appear at the end of the summer when other plants are dying back.

LEFT *Solanum crispum* 'Glasnevin', the Chilean potato tree, is a strong, fast-growing climber. From June through to September, it produces a mass of mauve-blue flowers with yellow stamens that set off the dark green leaves. In the autumn these are followed by tiny, yellow-white berries, which are poisonous. Tie the stems onto a trellis or wires to support its growth.

RIGHT *Tradescantia fluminensis*, or wandering Jew, can easily be grown in pots or hanging baskets and looks best in a group. There are several varieties, some of which are grown for their foliage, which might have a pinky purple blush or be striped with cream or silver. It is a perennial, flowering from April to November, and is easy to propagate.

ABOVE Philodendrons are evergreen, shade-loving plants that originate in South America. There are more than 350 different species, some of which have pink or red leaves, while others have red or bronze stems and young leaves. They prefer rainwater or room-temperature soft water, and are fast growing, so may need repotting annually.

RIGHT A sturdy wicker climbing frame has been provided for this *Clematis florida* var. *sieboldiana* to clamber up. From June to October, creamy white sepals surround deep purple petaloid stamens and open right back toward the stem. This plant, which will grow to 1.8–2.4m (6–8ft), needs to be kept warm and should do well in a conservatory.

OPPOSITE Another pretty corner with *Lapageria rosea*, or Chilean bellflower, and *Abutilon* used to good effect. Abutilons are sometimes known as flowering maples because of the shape of their leaves. Their long, lax flower stems can either be left to trail or trained up a wall. The bell–shaped flowers come in reds, oranges, and golds.

LEFT A pretty corner in the conservatory – attractive pots have been placed at ground level, and above and behind them, variegated ivies trail down to the ground, softening the outline of the ferocious–looking stone guardian of the door.

BELOW *Acacia dealbata*, or florists' mimosa, is a lovely tree of Australian origin. This well–known variety produces racemes of yellow pompoms in late winter or early spring and has attractive silvery grey, feathery leaves. Most acacias grow tall, but they can be controlled by being grown in containers and pruned when flowering is over.

Trailers

Trailing plants are not only elegant, they also have many practical uses. You could run a high-level shelf along one or more of the walls and place several trailers there to tumble forth and soften hard corners and empty wall space. Placed across a room, trailers can form a loose screen or divider. They also look good pouring over the side of a jardinière or a wall-mounted container, and you can use them to hide functional items such as wall sockets or the hosepipe tap. If you have a small, raised pond or other water feature, plants trailing and tumbling over the edge will soften the manmade outline.

In the summer, hanging baskets full of flowering plants cascading over the sides are always striking, and in winter fuchsias or petunias can be replaced with foliage plants, ivies, or tradescantia. Making up a basket of just a single colour and type of plant can produce a very effective statement. However, hanging baskets demand quite high maintenance and need plenty of water. If you have the right type of floor, buy an attachment for your hose for watering high-level pots or baskets. To avoid splashing the floor, use a ratchet device to move the baskets up and down.

RIGHT Traditionally, orchids were grown only by specialist collectors; these days, it is perfectly possible to grow several different kinds in the conservatory. Indeed, orchids are becoming ubiquitous, sold in every flower shop and supermarket. There are varieties that flower in winter, spring, and autumn, and the range of colours and patterns is wide. This one is an *Odontoglossum* hybrid.

Exotic plants

OPPOSITE This is a successful bougainvillea, with its mass of little cream flowers surrounded by papery bracts. Although they have hooks to help them climb, bougainvilleas need to be trained on wires or a trellis if you want them to cover a large space. They need direct sunlight and should be kept fairly dry in winter.

If you want to grow exotic, tropical plant species, you will need to have a very warm conservatory – at a minimum temperature of about 16°C (61°F), if possible – and keep the humidity up by misting or leaving pots of water in strategic positions.

Start with one or two key plants – striking, showy ones that will make focal points around which to grow smaller, background species. The bird-of-paradise plant, *Strelitzia reginae* (see page 96), is a good example and can grow to 1½m (5ft). The spiky orange-and-blue-petalled flowers emerge from the top of a bent green bract with a red stripe. These plants take a few years before they flower, but blooms then continue for several weeks. *Heliconia rostrata* has hanging scarlet bracts edged in green and tipped with yellow.

Bamboo, palms, orchids, or frangipani can add an Oriental touch, while bougainvillea, hibiscus, oleander, and mimosa bring the Mediterranean to mind. Decide what kind of look you are after and make sure all the plants you choose have more or less the same requirements of temperature and humidity. Remember that scent is important too, so try to include a few fragrant species, even if only a foliage plant such as a lemon verbena.

LEFT Hibiscus, a very popular plant for the conservatory, is available in an amazing range of colours from vivid reds to white with pink throats. Happy to receive plenty of sunshine and light, they still need protection from the heat of the midday sun. Prune in late winter to keep them a reasonable size.

ABOVE The bird-of-paradise plant, *Strelitzia reginae*, produces flowers that are truly flamboyant. It can be grown from seed but it takes up to six years to flower, so it is worth buying an established plant. Don't repot a mature plant: the growth restriction will force it to flower well.

LEFT Many, though not all, orchids are epiphytic – they grow above ground, on the branches of trees. Terrestrial orchids grow in light soil under trees, and both types prefer a moist atmosphere and shade from strong, direct sunlight. Moth orchids can flower for eight months of the year. Keep them moist but don't overwater them.

RIGHT *Brugmansia*, or angel's trumpet, is a glorious plant that has huge, trumpet-shaped flowers, several of which give off the most wonderful perfume. The larger species will grow into sizeable shrubs – in Southeast Asia they become fully grown trees. Water them freely and feed well and they will repay you with copious flowers all summer long.

BELOW *Plumbago auriculata* grows to about 3m (10ft) in a tub or container and produces clusters of beautiful blue flowers all summer long. It needs to be supported with wires or a trellis. Remove flowers as they finish, and cut it back hard in the early spring. The white form is also very attractive.

RIGHT If you want to achieve an exotic and jungly look without having to spend too much time caring for plants with special needs, try a mass of mixed foliage plants instead. Evergreen palms and ferns, both tall and short varieties, with dark green, red, or variegated leaves, will look good all year round.

Desert plants

Some people find cacti and succulents boring, but others absolutely love these curious
plants. A collection of cacti in a conservatory can look stunning, and as long as conditions
are right for them, they do not demand much attention. Both cacti and succulents come
in a variety of interesting, sculptural shapes, and you can group them together with a few
rocks and stones and some gravel to make your own little desert in your conservatory.

Cacti can form rosettes or barrels, have bodies like sea urchins, or large fan-like leaves,
and, periodically, and often surprisingly, will throw up flower spikes for your enjoyment.
Most of the growth of desert cacti takes place during the summer. Allow the top half of
the compost to dry out between watering times during the growth period, and during the
winter water them only two or three times. Because cacti are slow growing, use ordinary
fertilizer at quarter strength or buy a special cactus fertilizer.

One succulent, aloe, has extraordinary healing properties: cut a piece of leaf and
smear the sticky juice onto a burn. Continue until the pain stops and you will have little
or no blistering or scarring. It is also an effective remedy for scratches and rashes.

ABOVE Cacti and house leeks form the focus of
this table, showing how much can be fitted
into a fairly small, low bowl. As long as they
receive plenty of light and low humidity in
summer, and are not too warm over winter,
cacti will thrive. However, too much water
will cause root rot.

RIGHT *Mammillaria zeilmanniana*, the rose pincushion, is striking, particularly when its large purple-pink flowers appear in the summer. Others species in the genus produce pale yellow-and-red flowers.

BELOW LEFT In their natural habitat, cacti receive plenty of strong, direct sunlight and are exposed to low temperatures at night. They need to be planted in a ready-made cactus compost, or you can make your own by adding grit and peat to a soil-based compost.

BELOW RIGHT *Agave americana* and its variegated varieties are commonly known as the century plant. They make good container plants when young, but can grow as large as 1.8m (6ft), and their leaves are tipped with lethal spines.

Fruit and vegetables

There is something very satisfying about picking fruit and vegetables that you have grown yourself, and one of the joys of having a conservatory is being able to grow a few edibles, including fresh herbs, which you can have available for use all year long. It's a good way to interest children in gardening, too – they can eat as well as see the fruits of their work.

Tomatoes can be grown in tubs, and if you plant some pots of basil as well, you'll have one of the all-time great taste combinations. Chives, parsley, coriander, and mint are also easy to grow in pots – indeed, mint must be grown in a container as it is very invasive. Likewise, sweet and chilli peppers are easy and fun to grow – and very attractive too.

If you would like to grow fruit in your conservatory, visit a good nursery and ask for advice as to what you should buy. A grapevine or a fig may be too big, but you could try kiwi fruit or a pineapple plant, both of which need warmth all year round. Pineapples are fun to grow: next time you buy one, cut off the top, remove any soft flesh from it, and let it dry out for two days. Place it in a smallish pot of soil-based compost, water it minimally, and, after it has established a root system, give it a foliar feed from time to time.

ABOVE LEFT Peaches and nectarines do best in warm, sunny positions, and this fan-shaped peach tree is in just such a spot. Diligently trained and tended, it produces plenty of fruit. Both types of fruit tree are self-fertile, so only one tree is needed to obtain sufficient fruit for the average family.

ABOVE RIGHT To eat tomatoes through the autumn, strip the leaves from the plant and hang it in a cool, well-ventilated spot. Tomatoes will ripen about two weeks after picking, so just take a few each time. Put them in a bag with a ripe banana, and the gas that is given off will do the rest.

ABOVE LEFT Sow parsley seeds in late summer into a seed tray of peat-substitute compost after soaking them in warm water for a day. They germinate very slowly, but once large enough to handle, put them into 10cm (4in) pots, keep them out of direct sunlight, water regularly, and feed weekly with seaweed feed.

ABOVE RIGHT Like tomatoes and other fruiting vegetables, including aubergines (eggplants), peppers of various varieties are good to grow in containers in a conservatory as they are compact and mature quickly. Their bright colours ensure that they are as good to look at as they are to eat.

RIGHT An easy-to-grow yet spectacular vegetable, Swiss chard comes in an incredible range of brilliant hues – including pink, red, yellow, orange, white, and striped – and is highly nutritious.

Overwintering

Whether or not you need to overwinter plants will depend on where in the world you live. Northern climates are generally the coldest, but mountainous regions can also expect snowfall every winter. Even if the temperature never falls below freezing, you may need to bring some plants into the conservatory in seasons of torrential rain.

Bring in any plants that need protection from the change of season in good time – too much water can cause root and stem rot, and too much cold can be fatal. Most perennial plants need a bit of rest at some point during their year, so gradually reduce feeding and watering them, and try to keep them away from drafts. As many plants flower happily in winter, you will still have things of interest to look at during this time.

It is a sensible idea to have a good reference book handy so that you can find out exactly what conditions your plants should be kept in. Cacti need very little water in winter, amaryllis need three months with no water at all after their leaves start turning yellow, but begonias need moderate watering during this time. Try to please your plants and they will reward you handsomely.

Architectural plants

This kind of plant should really be the first type that you choose for your conservatory, whether you plan to have a large display or simply one or two pots or containers. A single dramatic specimen can either stand alone, filling an entire corner, or can be used as the focal point of a group of smaller, more delicate plants. It should be bold and striking, with either an architectural shape or extraordinary flowers or foliage. What you choose will depend partly on the style of your conservatory.

A Mediterranean-style conservatory would look best with plants such as bougainvillea or mimosa, while citrus trees in Versailles tubs or bay trees will suit a more classical style. Modern conservatories that are used as dining rooms or sitting rooms look very stylish with just one or two palms or bamboo, or choose an exciting flowering variety such as the bird-of-paradise plant or *Allamanda schottii* with its gorgeous golden flowers.

Most architectural plants are long lived, and by the time you acquire them they will represent several years of careful nurturing by the nursery gardener – hence the fact that they are quite expensive. View them as longterm investments and consider how big they

OPPOSITE This conservatory is kept both very warm and rather humid, as you can see from the healthy *Musa* (banana). The trunk of a banana plant is formed from its old leaves; just cut them off near the base when they begin to grow old and brown. The 'Dwarf Cavendish' variety will both flower and fruit, if conditions are right.

RIGHT This rectangular conservatory/sitting room makes very good use of architectural plants, which soften the lines of the room and look spectacular against the plain background. *Cyperus papyrus*, the papyrus plant, can grow to more than 4m (13ft) in height and was originally a wetland sedge used for papermaking in ancient Egypt.

OPPOSITE Although there are several different plants arranged around this dining and sitting room area, the eye is immediately drawn to the large palm with its arching fronds. Most palms need humidity, although the date variety will flourish in a hot and dry atmosphere. You can help them flourish by keeping the compost moist and by regular misting.

will grow and how much room their roots will need. Are you going to plant them in a bed or a container? Some architectural plants will grow into fully fledged trees if they are planted in a bed rather than a pot, so unless you are attempting to reproduce a jungle, you would be wise to restrict their growth and keep them healthy by regular feeding.

Palms make elegant additions to any style of conservatory, and as long as you do not let the temperature fall below the minimum that is recommended for your particular variety, they are reasonably easy to look after. They do like humidity, so make sure that you keep the leaves misted and the compost moist while they are in growth. Avoid drafts and sudden changes of temperature.

Kentia palms are probably the most popular type for growing in conservatories. *Howea forsteriana* has arching leaves made up of many leaflets arranged in pairs up the central leaf stalks. *Chamaedorea elegans*, native to Mexico, was very popular in Britain with the Victorians and is usually known as the parlour palm. These palms can tolerate shade but need protection from direct sunlight; remove older leaves as they turn brown.

LEFT The choice of containers plays an important role in the effective use of architectural plants, as does their positioning. In this large, formal, and very elegant space, two fig trees in pots raised on pedestals form a dramatic entranceway to the dining room from the conservatory.

The water garden

ABOVE Unusually, the main function of this conservatory is to house a pond for plants and fish. Two chairs and a table provide a quiet place to sit, talk, and watch and feed the fish. Other plants are contained in pots on windowsills and in a raised planting bed.

OPPOSITE This conservatory, full of lush green plants, has a raised stone pond with a fountain as its dramatic centrepiece. For such a feature to be effective, make sure that it suits the style, and matches the materials, of your conservatory. Here, both stonework and shape mirror those of the surrounding path.

Conservatories provide a source of pleasure for all the senses. Sight, smell, touch, taste, and sound can all play their parts, and a water feature not only looks lovely but also produces a wonderful sound. It will also increase humidity, which will help many plants to thrive.

You may decide upon a pond, either sunk into the floor or raised and surrounded by a wall. Perhaps a fountain would be more to your taste – a wide range is available from garden centres. Or you could even build a waterfall if you have the space.

A pool with a calm surface will reflect the plants growing in and around it, and if lit at night, will provide an eye-catching focus for your conservatory. Still water, essential for the cultivation of water lilies, brings potential algae problems, and moving water will need a small electric pump. A simple solution to the algae build up is to make a small water garden in a large pot or a lined, wooden half-barrel. If you grow the plants in containers, you can change both them and the water whenever you like. If you want to grow tropical water lilies or other tender aquatic plants, you will need to heat the water; seek specialist advice for this. Tropical lilies are available in many shades, and some bloom at night.

LEFT A small, Zen–style garden can look dramatic and peaceful but requires very little work. You can buy pebbles, stones, and rocks from garden centres – there is a good deal of choice in size and colour. Hollowed–out bamboo containers are simple, natural, and beautiful, and rosettes of cacti will add a little touch of colour.

Low-maintenance planting

In today's world, more and more of us have careers to think of as well as families to care for, and the time available for growing and nurturing plants in the conservatory is often limited. Many people also have a garden to contend with, so thought has to be given to how to use limited free time in the most useful way.

The obvious answer, both in the conservatory and the garden, is to choose plants that require little maintenance. Take advice from friends, read gardening books, and ask for suggestions from helpful and knowledgeable nurserymen. There are plenty of different low-maintenance plant species, suitable for a wide range of conditions, that you can make use of in your conservatory.

A collection of a specific type of plant could be what you need. Ferns, for example, will do well in a north-facing conservatory. They dislike direct sunlight, but do require humidity. A minimum temperature of 10–15°C (50–59°F), rising to 18°C (64°F) or more in the daytime, will suit them perfectly. Ferns can be small and ground-hugging or tall and statuesque, but as long as you keep them moist, they are fairly low maintenance.

ABOVE This pretty corner is full of plants that are reasonably trouble free, while still looking lush and green, and the Neptune fountain on the back wall ensures good humidity levels. Apart from watering and feeding the plants from time to time, you should keep them tidy by removing dead or dying leaves.

ABOVE RIGHT If you have a sunny south- or west-facing conservatory, palms and other sun-loving species are what you should aim for if you want low-maintenance plants. *Musa* (banana) always lends an air of exoticism, and many species will produce large, brightly coloured, heavy flowers and ornamental, though inedible, fruits.

Cacti and succulents are another group you can consider. Requiring similar temperatures in the conservatory they, unlike ferns, need lots of light and sunshine but otherwise are trouble free. They will need watering most in their growing season – two or three times a week in very hot weather – but in the winter, you will only need to water them every six weeks or so.

Spring bulbs, such as crocuses, hyacinths, narcissi, and tulips, are reasonably low maintenance and provide a cheerful splash of colour at just the right moment. Plant the bulbs in the autumn, give them a good watering, and then keep them in a cool, dark place, such as a garden shed or a garage, while they form their root system. Make sure that the soil does not dry out at any point and also check that the bulbs never become waterlogged or they will rot. When you see shoots appearing, bring them into the conservatory and watch them grow and flower. When their display is over, you can either plant them out in the garden or clean them off and keep them in a shady place until the following autumn, when you can pot them up again, using fresh potting soil each time.

4

Choosing furniture

Adding a conservatory to your house is quite different from adding an extension – a glazed roof and one or more glazed walls make the space not only lighter and brighter, but also make it feel halfway between indoors and out. Here you have the chance to use your imagination and to break away from the style you have created in the rest of the house with the type of furniture you choose.

A conservatory is so close to the natural world that it cries out to be furnished with natural materials regardless of whether you want to achieve classic formality, Moroccan Riad style, or a rustic Provençal haven. This is nothing new – if you look at old Victorian photographs and paintings of conservatories, the furniture is usually made of wicker or cast iron. In the late 1800s, when middle-class Victorians were busily adding conservatories onto their houses, they were inspired by the architecture that they had seen on their travels abroad, and wanted furniture that was light, elegant, comfortable, and strong enough to hold up well in humid conditions.

As traders came and went around the world, a fashion for Oriental exoticism was born, and bamboo and cane furniture from the Far East began making its way back to Europe and North America. European manufacturers soon caught on to these new ideas and imported the materials with which to make their own creations until the cultivation of the appropriate plants was established in various European countries. Hunt around auction houses and architectural salvage places for old conservatory furniture – it is still

ABOVE The deck chairs set the scene in this snug, informal space and the upholstered sofa at one end, with its mass of cushions, looks very inviting. The addition of a few side tables, a reading lamp, and old orangey yellow rugs on the floor help to make the room both bright and warm looking, both during the daytime and at night.

PREVIOUS PAGE Metal is a popular material choice for conservatory furniture, particularly for a dining or breakfast room. Along with the stone floor, these simple chairs and table give this space a stylish and rather formal look. The seat pads not only provide comfort but can be changed easily to create a different look.

RIGHT Despite being all white – furniture, flooring, and walls – this dining room looks elegant and peaceful rather than cold. This is the sort of scheme that can work in a conservatory, which receives more natural light than an enclosed room. The natural-wood roof timbers and wooden picture frames on either side of the dresser add warmth.

BELOW A small, informal sitting area has been designed in this conservatory. The wicker sofa and chair are both painted appropriately, and the seat and back cushions go very well together despite not being exactly the same fabric. Wicker furniture of this design takes up a fair amount of space, but it is light and easily moved around.

possible, though pricey, to find original Victorian plant stands and other pieces; Edwardian pieces are available, too, at quite reasonable prices.

There are, of course, an enormous number of places to look for modern and reproduction conservatory furniture – get in touch with specialist shops and spend time poring over their brochures, visit good department stores and garden centres, or look on eBay. You can use the Internet to locate specialist auctions, too – there is an antique garden furniture show in the New York Botanical Garden every year, for example, and house and garden trade fairs are held in most countries.

When deciding on the style of your conservatory furniture and the material from which it is made, bear in mind that it will need to be resistant to bright light, heat, and humidity, as well as being low-maintenance and easy to keep clean. When conservatories began their resurgence in the 1970s, the prevailing look was for everything to match. Happily, style ideas have loosened up since then, and a selection of furniture in different designs and materials, chosen with care, can look both stylish and relaxed.

RIGHT Who would not want to sit in this conservatory looking out onto the lake? The natural colours of the wooden frame and stone floor are continued in the natural wood tables, and the blue of the water is picked out around the arms and back of the two basket chairs.

OPPOSITE There is a lovely, old-fashioned look to this room that reminds me of the conservatory at my grandmother's cottage. The open weave of the canes in the chairs and the simple, low table look just right here, and there is plenty of room to have a cup of tea and a cucumber sandwich while admiring the gardener's green-fingered talent.

Living in the conservatory

Perhaps unlike in the other rooms in your house, you can make whatever you want of your conservatory. People most commonly use this space, however, as a living room – perhaps a family room. A range of options is available, to suit all situations. Here, you can relax with the newspaper over a cup of coffee, help the kids with their homework, gossip with a friend over a glass of wine, read a book, play card games, or listen to music late at night.

Living rooms are multifunctional and so will need to contain various items of furniture, including comfortable chairs, a sofa or two (or even a chaise longue), a coffee table, perhaps a foot stool or ottoman, and possibly a small dining or card table with a couple of upright chairs. And don't forget to consider allowing for at least one or two small side tables as well – after all, you will need somewhere to put your small items.

Storage tends to be overlooked in a conservatory, but if you are going to use this room as much as it deserves, you will need practical places in which to clear things out of the way. The only problem is the shortage of solid walls against which to place cabinets and

LEFT The corner of this Gothic-style conservatory is full of plants and furniture. The slatted wooden garden chair has a checked cushion on the seat for added comfort, and the check theme is continued with further cushions and the tablecloth. The wicker seats form a sofa if pushed together, but can easily be moved apart to form two separate seats when necessary.

chests, or on which to hang shelves or wall cupboards. It may be possible to fit storage seats against the low walls around the edges of your conservatory, or to find low storage pieces that won't block the windows. Be inventive – use blanket boxes as coffee tables and small chests of drawers as side tables, so that unnecessary clutter can be kept to a minimum.

In a room that doubles as a home office, there are other furniture considerations. You will require a work table of some sort – perhaps a roll-top desk, a bureau, or a modern glass-and-metal table – together with shelving, cupboards or cabinets, and possibly a plan chest and/or an easel, if you are an artist, a designer, or an architect. If you will be entertaining clients, you may also need to allow space for a more relaxed area with a low table and a couple of comfortable chairs.

To cater for teenage children, and when there's enough space for a larger conservatory, you may want to think about accommodating a table-tennis table, or even a pool or snooker table. Although you will need to make sure that you have the toughest glazing available in case of accidents, this is nevertheless a perfectly feasible option.

OPPOSITE This Gothic-style room has been specifically designed as the main sitting room of the house. Fitted carpets are not usually laid in conservatories because of their proximity to the great outdoors. However, in climates where the weather is guaranteed to be pleasant for a large part of the year, little debris will be brought into the house from the patio. The upholstered furniture is protected from bleaching by the roof blinds.

Alternatively, for a conservatory that's used as a second, living room, you may want to accommodate books, statues, vases of flowers, glassware, or other objects, in built-in or free-standing shelving against the solid wall of the house. This wall is also useful for hanging photographs or paintings – but be aware of the orientation of your conservatory. The more direct sunlight it gets, the more likely it is that photos and artworks will bleach, and the same applies to paintings and the spines of books.

In addition to furniture, in any conservatory you will no doubt want to accommodate at least a few plants in pots and/or baskets. For this, try to find containers that complement the overall style of the room – Classical stone urns in a traditional conservatory, for example, or minimal stainless steel in a more modern room.

Before buying any furniture it is essential that you consider the overall size and shape of the space. There is no point in falling for a beautiful, large, Indian swing chair, for example, if you will be unable to move around it easily and there will be nowhere for anyone else to sit. If necessary, draw up a scaled floor plan of the space on graph paper,

ABOVE **Wickerwork tables and chairs come in all sorts of shapes and sizes. They are also available in many different colours. If you can't find exactly the shade you want, buy them in their natural state and paint them yourself. If you become bored with subtle, muted tones, you can add a splash of colour.**

RIGHT **A modern daybed or chaise longue is a perfect piece of furniture for a conservatory, if you have the space for one. Seat and back cushions are essential if you have dreams of spending the afternoon lying on it with a book.**

OPPOSITE **One of the great things about wicker furniture is its versatility. It is easy to think of it in a traditional country setting, but it also combines well with modern pieces and can look very stylish. In this huge space, its use adds warmth to the otherwise cool neutral colour scheme, while its texture contrasts with the smooth stone floor and white walls.**

showing doors, windows, and potential obstructions such as radiators and plug sockets. Cut scaled drawings of the furniture you require out of paper and move them around on the floor plan until you are happy with the arrangement. Remember that circulation space is just as important as seating room. You may even wish to cut life-sized plans of the furniture out of news- or brown paper and lay them on the floor in the room itself. That way, you can walk around them and really get a feel of how the room will work before spending any money.

Whatever furniture you choose, it should be functional as well as comfortable, so that your new conservatory immediately becomes the place in your home where you will want to spend quality time, whether alone, or with your family and friends. Cane, wood, and metal are, generally speaking, the best materials for conservatory furniture. Practical, relatively inexpensive, and good-looking cane furniture – made from woven willow, rattan, or bamboo – is many people's first choice. It has a pleasing, natural feel, though can sometimes be rather bulky. It is also a sustainable material and is available in a wide

ABOVE **This modern, rectangular conservatory, has unusual retro-style furniture. Robust fabric is lashed onto the wooden frames of the chairs at both ends, allowing the seat to swing free in exactly the same way as a traditional deck chair; however, these seats are solid and do not fold flat. The room is furnished as an informal living area in which to watch movies and listen to music.**

range of designs, from traditional to modern. Cane can be left in its natural finish, or it can be bleached, stained, or painted to blend or contrast with your chosen colour scheme. Add cushions to seats for extra comfort, and a glass top to tables to give a flat surface.

An interesting variation on cane is "Lloyd Loom" furniture. In 1917, the American Marshall Burns Lloyd invented a new technique of wrapping wire with woven paper, weaving it on a loom and upholstering it onto bentwood frames. The result, though similar in appearance, was stronger and less likely to splinter than cane. Lloyd Loom furniture was, and continues to be, extremely popular, and not only are early pieces still to be found but many of the original designs continue to be made. Early Lloyd Loom furniture is highly sought after and fetches large prices at specialist auctions. It is not really, therefore, for casual use in a conservatory. However, the modern versions are more affordable. There are a plethora of companies selling "Lloyd Loom", from sofas and side tables to dining chairs and chaise longues, in styles both classic and surprisingly contemporary. Lloyd Loom of Spalding still makes pieces in the United Kingdom to Marshall Burns Lloyd's original processes.

Wooden furniture is another versatile choice for a living-room conservatory. While upright wooden chairs are best kept for dining, benches with cushioned seats provide a pretty, practical alternative to a conventional sofa, and wooden steamer chairs can be very comfortable. In a casual conservatory or a room that is dominated by plants, wooden garden chairs (perhaps with pretty seat pads) may be ideal as occasional seating. A wooden coffee table is a useful item of furniture, as is a side table, or maybe a butler's table – where the upper part is a detachable tray which rests on a folding base.

While metal furniture has great character and is eminently hard-wearing and durable, it tends to be rather cold and rigid. With squashy cushions, however, chairs can be made more comfortable, and, if this look suits you, it can be an excellent choice, successfully expressing the idea of blending outdoors and inside. It's best to avoid metal chairs and tables specifically designed for the garden, as they can look unsophisticated and clumsy; instead, opt for curly, decorative metalwork, which looks really attractive, especially when painted in a soft white or pastel shade.

LEFT Shown here is a long conservatory that lends itself to more than one seating area, with occasional tables, sofas, and chairs dotted about. The main area has a lovely old rug on the tiles, which lends a sense of comfort and warmth. The rattan furniture comes from Southeast Asia, and the rattan is woven across the entire frame of each chair, forming a skirt down to the floor.

ABOVE This beautiful conservatory is furnished with big squashy sofas in an elegant country style, making this a light, comfortable, and spacious room in which to relax. If you want to include upholstered pieces, choose hard-wearing fabrics in soft creams or pale shades that won't be bleached by sunlight. You can introduce colour with cheap and cheerful cushions if you wish.

Upholstered sofas and chairs are lovely to sink in to, but bear in mind that fabric (especially dark colours) will fade rapidly in strong sunlight, and if the room is at all humid the upholstery could become damp and mouldy. Provided this isn't a concern, you could choose whatever pieces suit your look – perhaps a casual, loose-covered sofa and chairs, or more formal, upright seating with button-backs and piped edgings. You could even opt for leather armchairs or beanbags – in fact, whatever furniture you would put in a conventional living room.

Certain types of conservatory furniture lends itself to creating a particular overall style, and it is worth keeping this in mind when buying and co-ordinating. Cane is perhaps the most versatile. It can, for example, be painted in pastel shades and accessorized with gingham or chintz fabrics for a pretty, rural look. Just add painted ceramics, botanical prints, delicate chandeliers, and vases of informally arranged flowers for a real English country feel. Alternatively, paint it white and add plain and checked cottons and linens, tongue-and-groove cabinetry, and simple floor and table lamps with pale fabric shades

LEFT The large conservatory shown here was built to provide a dining area and to open and brighten up the sitting room, and the décor is continued throughout the space. A flamboyant mixture of traditional and Art Deco, set off with a large, metal-and-glass Moroccan lantern, the styling of this room is surprisingly effective.

for a cool, New England look. Otherwise, go for an exotic, Far Eastern effect by accessorising with wooden boxes with large brass handles, woven baskets, carved-stone Buddhas or elephants, paper lanterns, and carved-wooden mirrors.

The plainer types of metal furniture can appear unfussy and functional – ideal for a simple lean-to conservatory, perhaps. On the other hand, curly metal has a wonderfully French look: if you want to go the whole hog, team it with toile-de-Jouy fabrics, old metal café signs, oversized chocolate mugs, painted wall clocks, and enamelware with French lettering. Or, for a typically classic English feel, go for casual upholstered furniture, adding personal touches such as books, vases, plates and bowls, lamps, rugs, assorted cushions, galvanized-metal watering cans, wooden trugs, and so on, for an eclectic mix. Nothing need be too new or pristine, as this look is all about comfortable informality.

In any conservatory used for relaxation, you may want to install some kind of music system. At the most basic level, you can easily use a portable CD player, or an MP3 player with a pair of speakers, to meet your musical needs. Alternatively, you might choose to

OPPOSITE You can see at a glance that this is a conservatory for people with a keen interest in gardening. This is the way into the house from the garden, and it is full of attractive and fascinating clutter. It is sensible to have placed a table and chairs here to sling a coat on, or to sit and pore over a plant book.

RIGHT This wooden lean-to serves various functions, including providing access to three different parts of the house. Furnished comfortably, it is a good place to sew or knit, or just rest and read a book. You could even put up an unexpected guest here if you already had a house full.

OPPOSITE This rattan steamer chair is made in two separate parts – the main body of the chair has a fairly long seat and useful arms upon which to place your drink or magazine. The additional footstool can be pulled fully forward to allow its occupant to stretch out, or it can be stored underneath. Alternatively, remove it altogether, add a cushion, and you have a seat for someone else.

have a couple of speakers connected to the main stereo system in the house. If you are very keen on hi-fi, though, you should consult a specialist dealer while you are still planning your conservatory because you will need to allow for a dedicated sound system, complete with wireless networking and concealed speakers. Don't forget to give careful consideration as to how you will store CDs, if that is the format of your music collection.

Many people see their conservatory as a place of peace and quiet, removed from the intrusive sounds of everyday life. Yet a conservatory can be an ideal place to watch television, and if this appeals you may wish to consider a flat-screen television with a plasma or LCD (liquid crystal display) screen. These are the least obtrusive option (you can even get versions that are built in to mirrors, or that have customized covers to suit your decorative scheme), but they can be costly. The alternative would be to think about building a TV into a cupboard, or mounting it on a wall bracket so that it doesn't take up vital floor space. The same applies to other technology, such as DVD and video players, satellite boxes, home computers, and so on.

LEFT As you can see, this kitchen was rather small and much less bright before the conservatory was added. The new space has been made into a comfortably relaxed eating area that looks onto the garden. The simple wooden table and director's chairs are separated from the kitchen area by a wooden chopping block.

Cooking in the conservatory

If you are someone who reads newspapers and watches television, you could be forgiven for being under the impression that kitchens and cooking are going out of style. We are constantly being told that families rarely eat together any more, and that cooking today means heating ready-cooked meals in a microwave oven. The number of cookery and food-related shows on television somewhat belies that theory, however, and in many households, the kitchen is still the focus of family life.

A great many houses and apartments have kitchens that are too small to eat in, however, and some apartments have tiny, galley kitchens in which there is room for only one person at a time. The desire for a larger, brighter kitchen may be your reason for wanting a conservatory, but there are a few practical problems that you will need to be aware of, and to find solutions for, before you order and/or build it.

The first problem is humidity. Kitchens are places where a great deal of moisture is generated – cooking and washing dishes unavoidably produce moisture – and, particularly during the winter in northern climes, when humid air hits cold glass, condensation is

formed. Condensation in a conservatory can cause serious problems – mould can begin to develop on the blinds and on the walls, and even on the glass. If the situation persists for any length of time, fabrics will begin to rot, and the whole room will begin to smell and feel unpleasant.

There are ways of avoiding this problem, however. Firstly, your glazing will need to have as good insulating qualities as possible to minimize condensation, and, secondly, you will need to have very good ventilation. If you live in a temperate climate, you will not want to keep your doors and windows open too often in winter, so you will need to incorporate roof vents and extractor fans as well as the obligatory trickle vents at the top of the windows. Place the extractor fans close to the source of moisture to ensure its speedy removal, and try to reduce the overall moisture level in the house by fitting extractor fans in your bathrooms and lavatories – and in your utility room, too, if you have one. If you can possibly avoid keeping the washing machine in the kitchen, do so: there may be enough room to put elsewhere in the home.

ABOVE **This stylish work station has a polished-granite work surface and a small, circular sink in which to wash vegetables. It also houses an oven with a convenient drawer beneath it in which to keep roasting dishes and baking trays. Cupboards to either side of the oven, as well as at the rear of the station, provide generous storage space.**

The second problem is the amount of storage space that is needed in a kitchen. In a conservatory, you may have only one solid wall against which you can place cupboards and shelves, and you will want your refrigerator to stand against a solid wall as well. However, as long as you have dwarf walls of about 1m (3¼ft) high, you will be able to hide hobs and sinks, and install low-level cupboards and shelving so that they cannot be seen from the outside.

Glazing should start at the level of the worktop, so that you can enjoy the view when preparing food, cooking, and washing the dishes. In a conservatory kitchen, you can be sure of good natural light, and you can add all kinds of other lights, not only over the preparation and cooking area but also to the underside of wall-hung cupboards and inside those at a low level. If your conservatory has a wooden frame, you will have plenty of places to fix higher-level shelving or a circular or semi-circular saucepan rack as well as cup hooks.

Another option is to arrange all your shelving, storage cupboards, and worktop as a central island – if necessary, you could have a hob and an oven there too, but you might

ABOVE Here, the work station is placed in order to separate the kitchen area from the dining room. As well as an oven and a sink, there are drawers and cupboards here. The wooden surface can be used for making pastry as well as for general food preparation, while the butcher's block at the end is for chopping.

RIGHT The lovely country-kitchen style of the table and chairs suits this room very well. The natural wood-topped table stands on good solid legs, painted white, and the drawer contains the place mats when they are not in use. The chairs are modern but of a traditional style, with comfortable rush seats.

LEFT Here the kitchen wall has been removed and a conservatory dining room-cum-living room added that is the width of the rear, paved garden. The two remaining solid walls can carry paintings and the radiator, which has a decorative cover. The round pedestal table has just sufficient room beneath it to pull up four basket chairs – not in view, the matching pair are in the living room area.

have problems with a hood for the hob. Many cooker hoods have an integrated extractor fan, which is especially important in a mainly glass kitchen.

There are all sorts of materials with which to make your worktop. Wood, slate, granite, and marble all have their place, as do manmade materials such as Corian, a DuPont product, with which you can even have an integral sink unit. Hygienic and non-porous, Corian is available in more than one hundred shades and is both robust and easy to maintain. Natural materials will often be best in a traditional-style kitchen, while manmade ones can be used for a modern, hi-tech look. A kitchen design specialist will be able to help you work out the best solution for your needs and style of kitchen.

Even if your conservatory kitchen is quite small, try to leave a shelf or windowsill on which you can grow a few herbs. In the middle of winter, you will be glad that you don't have to trudge out to the garden in search of a few mint leaves that have not succumbed to frost, and you can keep warmth-loving herbs, such as basil, growing all year round in the kitchen, if you stagger planting.

OPPOSITE ABOVE This conservatory kitchen faces south, and needs blinds that are fitted to the whole of the roof glazing and kept drawn at the height of the sun to keep the room cool, although sunlight still filters through. Most of the kitchen appliances and cupboards are against the one solid wall; the station in the centre, with its in-built chopping block and sink, gives additional storage space.

OPPOSITE RIGHT In this small, terraced property, the back wall of the existing north-facing kitchen has been opened up and a simple, lean-to conservatory added. The new kitchen is in the conservatory, and a wooden breakfast bar forms the divider between the new and old space. Good ventilation is needed, but blinds are not necessary here.

Dining in the conservatory

Many of us live in houses that do not have a separate dining room, and we make do with a dining table in the kitchen or in the living room. Conservatories, however, make great dining rooms and are fantastic places in which to entertain. What could be nicer than eating under the stars, perhaps by candlelight, or enjoying an informal afternoon tea overlooking the garden?

Before thinking about types and styles of furniture for your conservatory dining room, it's important to plan ahead. What will you use the room for? A small space for a light snack will need different furniture than a grander area for large dinner parties. What is the maximum number of guests you are likely to entertain? Once you know how many people you need to seat, you can work out a measurement for your table and chairs. Don't forget that there will need to be enough space for people to pull the chairs in and out easily without feeling cramped. And how much storage do you need? Unless you are going to keep everything in the kitchen, you may also want to allow room for a dresser, sideboard, or similar piece of furniture in which you can keep china, cutlery, table cloths,

and napkins, and that will provide you with a surface on which to put serving dishes, a bowl of fruit, or wine bottles and glasses. If in doubt about what furniture you can fit in, or how to arrange it, draw up a scaled floor plan and play around with it until you get it right.

If your conservatory dining room is spacious, there'll be an endless choice of furniture to suit all budgets. However, if space is at a premiumyou may have to play a few clever tricks. You could, for example, buy a gate-leg table that folds down when not in use, or invest in one that incorporates separate leaves that can be used to extend it when you have company. Glass-topped tables, or ones made from slender metal or from see-through acrylic, will have the effect of making the space seem larger, as will pale colours, simple shapes, and a lack of clutter. You may even wish to consider stacking or folding chairs – or simply make do with bringing extra chairs in from the garden or from other rooms when necessary. Remember that a dining table whose shape echoes that of the conservatory itself makes the most economical use of space.

ABOVE **This spacious, two-storey conservatory dining room has been separated from the kitchen area by the addition of a spiral staircase to the upper floor, and receives full sunlight when the roof blinds are not drawn. The retro-style, metal-framed chairs have had both seat and back cushions added for extra comfort.**

LEFT **A lovely dining area has been arranged in this conservatory that has doors opening onto the lovely country garden all around it. Wire chairs, with added seat cushions can be drawn up to the table top, which rests on central metal legs; they can easily be moved onto the patio outside. The whole feeling is one of lightness and proximity to the garden.**

ABOVE A stylish, formal, modern dining room has been made in this garden room with its traditional black-and-white tiled floor. Glazed walls and a large roof lantern make it a good space for plants as well as for the elegant wire chairs and circular metal table. The chandelier, centred over the table, will throw a pleasantly soft light over diners in the evening.

Most conservatory dining rooms adjoin or extend from the kitchen, and as such it makes sense to choose furniture that, in style, colour, and material, complements that of your kitchen, ensuring a smooth transition from one room to another. If you have a farmhouse-style kitchen, for example, you might choose a rustic oak dining table and a set of rush-seated, ladder-back chairs for the conservatory; with a classic kitchen you might want a dark-wood table and upholstered chairs; and next to a modern kitchen, you might like a glass-topped table and coloured-plastic chairs. The principle of complementary styles is particularly important where the adjacent conservatory and kitchen are open-plan to one another – you should aim to make the two areas feel separate yet still related. And if you are not keen on the idea of the kitchen being in view at all times, you could use beaded curtains or a cane or wooden screen to create a visual break; a row of hanging baskets full of trailing plants, or a shelf with pots of trailers, work the same way. You may even have sufficient space to place a couple of comfortable chairs between the kitchen and dining areas, so friends to sit and talk to you as you cook.

OPPOSITE The white-painted table and chairs shown here form an attractive and practical family eating area. Made to a traditional design, the chairs have rush seats and do not need cushions. Easily maintained, this table requires only a pretty cloth added to it when guests are coming to dine.

RIGHT This spacious, formal dining room in America is north facing and surrounded on three sides by woodland and garden. The large veneered table and upholstered chairs do not receive too much direct sunlight, but even so, the table should be protected in the daytime. The heavy chandelier has electric candle bulbs cradled between the antlers from which it is formed and is hung from the central beam, making an unusual talking point.

BELOW Another lovely dining room in a modern, lean-to conservatory, this one has 180-degree views over an Italian valley and the hills beyond. Black-and-white marble floor tiles visually separate the dining area from the kitchen, and white voile blinds on the windows can be pulled down to soften the harsh glare of the sun during the afternoon. The glass-topped table and wooden chairs with decorative open basketwork on the back are both elegant and practical.

The dining table is the focal point of this room, and sets the scene for everything else in it. For a stunning focalpoint you could choose a polished or veneered wooden table – though these are best kept to north-facing rooms, where direct sunlight is less liable to cause damage. In any case, it is a good idea to cover a table such as this during the daytime – there are brand-name felts that are specifically designed to protect furniture. Simply put a pretty cloth over the top, and the table will come to no harm during the day; at night, remove the cover and set the table as usual.

If you prefer furniture that is practical and easy to maintain, look for a natural wood table. Oak ages rather beautifully, and soft woods, such as pine, can be limed to produce an interesting effect. You could just as easily buy a very ordinary wooden table from your local junk shop and paint it or cover it with some gorgeous fabric.

Wood is by no means the only choice for tables. A thick slab of glass gives a sleek, modern look, while a stone or marble top on a wrought-iron base can look elegant and classic. Other options include metal, ceramic, slate, mosaic, or even Moroccan zellig,

which is a simplified and less expensive form of mosaic. Rattan or bamboo are traditional, but remember that you will need to add a glass top to give a level surface.

As for seating, wooden chairs look best around a wooden table, but natural-wood tables can also look fine with metal chairs around them. If your table top is made of another material, consider wirework, iron, aluminium, or steel chairs in either a modern or a traditional design. Because metal is both hard and cold to sit on, however, you will need to add seat cushions, with or without ties. Such cushions are very widely available, but make sure that tthey are washable and that the fabric is robust enough to stand up to conservatory conditions.

Your conservatory dining room may open onto a patio area and this can be a great bonus during good weather. You could have a barbecue outside on the patio and bring the grilled food in to eat at the dining table, or enjoy a pre- or post-dinner drink with your guests there. Make the most of the fact that you have an indoor-outdoor area and enjoy it to the fullest.

ABOVE This small Mediterranean patio space has been glazed over to afford the owners year-round use. Plenty of sunshine allows plants to decorate the otherwise fairly plain space, and the wooden table and chairs suit the local style. The table top is usually protected by a cloth during the day to prevent sun damage.

OPPOSITE While this room cannot be called a dining room as such, it is certainly a snug and pretty spot in which to eat breakfast or take tea in the afternoon. The old bentwood table is covered with a crocheted cloth, and the bamboo and cane chairs look comfortable. A bamboo blind above the table allows the sun to filter through while ensuring that the table remains pleasantly shaded.

5

Finishing touches

The finishing touches to your conservatory deserve as much thought as everything else – attention to detail can make or break your new space. By this stage, you will already have invested a substantial amount of time and money in the project, so try not to stint with window dressings or lighting. You might also think about including a water feature or buying a piece sculpture for extra decorative effect.

Deciding on the decor of your new space is both exciting and creative – this is where your ideas come to life and you really make your mark. You know exactly how you are going to use this room, and you have very firm ideas as to how you want it to look – you are onto the last lap. Your colour scheme will be in place and you will know what sort of furniture you are going to use, so now you need to think about the last few things to dress the space and finish off the whole scheme.

Good quality door and window furniture may not sound very thrilling, but it makes quite a difference. You can aquire well-made brass fitments either new, from any number of specialist shops, or reconditioned from architectural salvage companies. Ironware is available too, in different styles, and doorknobs and escutcheon plates (ornamental or protective plates for keyholes) are also found in wood, porcelain, and ceramic.

Even if you are not going to use your conservatory for serious gardening, you will want a few plants, and absolutely any plant will look so much better once it has been transferred from its depressing-looking plastic pot into a different container. Pots can be plain or decorative, old or new, hand-made or mass-produced. Most are made from terracotta or ceramic, but lead and aluminium containers are also available. Pots are made all over the world - look out for examples from North Africa and southern Europe as well as the gorgeously decorated glazed Chinese ones. Antique containers are increasingly difficult and expensive to aquire – they have attracted the attention of major auction houses, with predictable effects on their price – but they can still be found if you are prepared to search widely.

PREVIOUS PAGES The conservatory shown here has been added on to a rather dark dining room. Guests can sit here with a drink whilst they look at the menu and wait for their table. The wooden flooring has been extended throughout, giving continuity, and Venetian blinds fitted on all the windows and doors, together with roof blinds, give both shade and a sense of privacy.

BELOW Pinoleum blinds have been used to shade the roof, doors, and windows in this rather formal conservatory sitting room, and the photograph gives a good sense of the diffused light that filters through them. A mixture of wall lights and standard lamps forms the lighting scheme, and the ceiling fan helps keep the room cool in warm weather.

ABOVE The roof of this conservatory has been glazed with opaque glass, thus avoiding the need for blinds while providing some protection from the sun. The windows are clear, and because the room affords long views over open countryside, blinds have not been installed. The colours of the furniture and floor warm up the look of the room.

ABOVE RIGHT The arrangement of pleated fabric blinds on the windows and of curtains on the doors made from the same material softens the look of the sitting room here. A large mat placed by the doors to the garden helps to protect the fitted carpet from leaves and debris brought into the house.

Look around for a *jardinière* or flowerpot holder, or an *étagère* – tiered shelves – both made of wire, upon which to display your plants. Alternatively have something custom-made in metal or wood to fit an awkward angle or particular position. Urns are another possibility: often made of cast stone or lead and placed upon, or sometimes an integral part of, a pedestal, they are a lovely way to show off trailing plants. Formal wooden Versailles tubs look at their best with citrus trees in them, or you could go for half barrels or smaller tubs or troughs.

The point is that the more effort you make with even the smallest of decorative elements in your conservatory, the happier you will be in the end. Of course you will be longing for it all to be finished, for the curtains or blinds to be in place, and the door and window furniture installed, to have found that piece of sculpture and to be able to use and enjoy it all. Don't worry if it isn't completely perfect to begin with – like any other room, you will need to live in it for a while, and tweak it here and there, before you are satisfied.

RIGHT The curtains in this conservatory have been fixed to the highest point of the roof and then draped to the sides, where a curtain rail has been installed. The problem with this arrangement is that in order to shade the roof, all the curtains need to be drawn. Although this looks pretty, it would be much more practical to have separate operating systems for roof and window shades.

OPPOSITE Curtains have been used to good effect in this elegant Italian dining area. Swathes of muslin front curtains in a heavy fabric allow privacy when they are drawn while still giving a light and airy appearance. The doors can be opened onto the garden, making this a pleasant place to eat.

Blinds and curtains

Most people find that they need to install blinds or curtains of some description in a conservatory, partly to give themselves and their plants some shade and partly to give themselves some privacy. The choice of options is huge.

There are specialist manufacturers who will make blinds for unusually shaped windows, but of course they are expensive. If you need to take this route, make sure you know exactly what you are buying. There should be a guarantee, but for how many years will it last? Will the blinds both keep the heat at bay during the summer and help to prevent heat loss during the winter? Will they allow sufficient light to reach your plants? Are they fire retardant and mould resistant? How easy are they to clean? These are all points to be taken into consideration.

Blinds can be installed both internally and externally, although the latter option is the most costly because these blinds have to stand up to all sorts of weather conditions. Although external blinds are extremely effective at preventing heat from reaching the conservatory, they often trap leaves and twigs and are difficult to keep clean. On the other hand, if you are a serious gardener, it might be well worth thinking about external blinds, because interior ones would be an obstacle to training climbers to grow across the interior of the roof.

Externally fitted blinds are usually the wooden Venetian kind, which can be automatically controlled to alter the angle of the slats according to the angle of the sun. If the roof is a straightforward shape, such as a lean-to or a ridged, blinds made of linked wooden slats, often cedar, can be fitted as an external roller blind that just unfurls down the length, or draws back into a roll at the top. Venetian blinds are also available in aluminium. The heavy-duty slats have reinforced edges and can be either manually or electrically operated.

It is also possible to buy fabric awnings for external use. Made of mesh or acrylic, they are hard-wearing and useful. Although acrylic ones are often more decorative, mesh awnings are more effective, because you can see out through them, yet they provide a good level of shading and heat rejection. Awnings are mounted flush with the glazing and run up and down guides that are fitted to the glazing bars. They retract into a headbox and are almost always electrically controlled.

Interior blinds can be made of fabric, cane, bamboo, pinoleum, wood, or aluminium. Roller blinds made of fabric are probably the least expensive type to buy, and they are also simple to use and easy to clean. Backed with aluminium, they can help control heat loss and gain. The tighter the blinds are fitted, the more the heat will be trapped between the fabric and the glass, throwing some of the heat back through the glass instead of letting

ABOVE **These wooden Venetian blinds give this Mediterranean conservatory a clean, contemporary look. Venetian blinds can be made to fit any shape of window, and motorized controls alter the angle of the louvres as well as closing and opening the blinds. The striped shadow that is thrown across the rear of the room is visually appealing.**

LEFT **Some effort has gone into finding a period lamppost for use as a structural support for the roof of this wide, lean–to conservatory dining and sitting room. Bamboo blinds in the roof provide shade and, together with the many palms and banana plants, provide a tropical feel to the space.**

RIGHT Pinoleum blinds are the traditional material for use in conservatories. Made from tiny strips of sawn pine sewn together and finished with edges of cloth, these blinds are less likely to sag than most other fabrics and, as you can see here, they can be made to fit awkward roof shapes.

BELOW The apex of this double-height conservatory has been raised above the natural roofline of the house in order to achieve the required area for the dining/ sitting room. Windows for high-level ventilation have been installed to join the new roof level to the old one. Blinds cover the whole of the south-facing roof.

it all into the conservatory. Tensioned roller blinds do have one drawback, however – they roll up so fast that they often squash unsuspecting insects as they go, so make sure you give them a quick shake before you close them.

Pleated fabric blinds are also very popular and are easy to clean with a vacuum cleaner. It is easy to have solar reflective finishes applied to this kind of blind, but they are best fitted to windows and doors rather than to roofs. They can be operated manually or mechanically, but the latter is preferable: with manual blinds you will have swathes of string pull cords between windows, and this not only looks unsightly but can also be potentially dangerous if there are young children in the house.

Cane or bamboo blinds look very attractive, especially in an older style of conservatory, and are a good choice if you are using furniture made of similar materials. Pinoleum blinds, which have been in use since c.1860, are made of fine strips of wood woven to different degrees of tightness to allow more or less light through. Available in a variety of colours, they soften a room with pretty, dappled light.

Another alternative is to use Venetian blinds, either made of wood or aluminium. The horizontal louvres are adjustable and can be controlled by an electric motor, which also opens and closes them. Venetian blinds can be used on windows and doors, as can simple, vertical-strip blinds. An increasingly popular choice is to have the glazing made with the blinds in place in the cavity. This means you have no cleaning worries, and it is an efficient method of keeping out the heat.

Curtains can be used in a conservatory, but look best when the fabric is something fine and light, such as muslin or voile, which, hung generously, create a floaty, ethereal look and give a lovely diffused light. Heavy curtains are not appropriate for most conservatories, although they can work well in a sunroom. You can always choose a combination of materials and types of blind or curtain – pinoleum for the roof and muslin for the windows, for example. Sometimes, particularly when there are issues of privacy, curtains for the windows may be just what you need, but try to aim for lighter fabrics and colours that you can scoop back with an attractive cord or tie, rather than heavy, dark fabrics that will not look appropriate during the daytime.

ABOVE There is a wide variety of blinds to choose from, as well as different operating systems. This picture shows how neatly a Roman blind folds up when it is retracted. This one is operated manually, as you can see from the cord hanging beside it, but motorized controls can be installed.

RIGHT and OPPOSITE Pale-grey pinoleum blinds have been installed on both the roof and the walls and doors give the room an air of muted elegance. The soft, dappled light that filters through is very easy on the eye and provides protection for both people and plants.

LEFT Opaque-glass side walls afford some privacy, when this modern conservatory dining room is in use, although it is still overlooked by first floor of the house next door. The arched, steel wall lamp provides the main light for diners, while the candles are more for decoration than practicality.

Lighting

How you design your lighting scheme will depend on what you plan to do with the room: different functions require different lighting solutions. The best idea is to use two or three lighting sources that can work for any situation, just as you would in any other room. Make sure that there are plenty of electrical sockets, ideally at different levels, including on the floor, so that you can move individual lamps to where they are most needed.

Lighting a glass room presents a different challenge from lighting any other room: uplighters and spots, for example, will give a harsh glare reflected from the roof glass, although the former can add a pleasant glow if they reflect onto a solid wall or under a projecting beam or shelf. Glass-walled rooms do not have nearly as many places available upon which to fix lights as rooms with solid walls, though most conservatories will have one or two solid walls as well as the glazing bars that can be used.

Small halogen lamps and lamp holders – individual or on tracks – are particularly suitable for conservatories because they take up very little space. Their fittings can be almost unnoticeable if they are fixed high in the roof, and they throw a good, bright light.

OPPOSITE This lovely conservatory, with its roof lantern for extra height, looks warm and inviting when seen from the outside in the evening. Lights have been placed at different levels within the room, throwing a soft glow. Controlled by a dimmer switch, the brightness can be increased as required, as it becomes darker outside.

ABOVE Matching chandeliers provide the
lighting in this pleasant, relaxed seating
area, which is mainly for use during the day.
Most chandeliers use electric candle bulbs,
but some, like these ones, have real candles.
Although candles throw a pretty light, it is
not bright, and there is always a potential
danger with naked flames.

A central chandelier and wall-mounted downlighters could be what you need, or you
could put in decorative brass or iron wall brackets, or hang lanterns. It is useful to install
a dimmer switch – the amount of light that you need early in the evening is probably
much more than you would like at midnight. Combined with standard lamps and table
lamps, all of these systems will provide you with plenty of flexibility.

LED (light-emitting diode) lights also have their place, both within the conservatory
and out in the garden. LEDs are the lights of the future. Very low-wattage lamps that
produce high light levels but no heat, they are expensive to buy but very long lasting.
They can be fitted flush to their surroundings for highly discreet lighting – place them at
a low level around the conservatory, and possibly around the base of the roof lantern, if
you have one. Alternatively, you might want to use them in more exciting ways – LED
rope lights come in a variety of colours, and you can wind them up columns or turn
them into modern chandeliers by twisting them around a frame made of metal coat
hangers, for example.

Bespoke conservatory manufacturers will certainly be able to offer you advice on lighting, but it is worth taking a look at a few specialist lighting shops and the lighting sections of good department stores, and also checking online, to give yourself a good idea of what is available and at what price.

Simple candles give a very soft and romantic light, although you need to be aware of the fire risk – both oil lamps and candles are possible sources of fire and should not be left unattended, particularly if there are children in the house. You can find very lovely candle shades in all sorts of styles from Shaker to Moorish, and there are any number of charming little coloured and etched glass holders for nightlights. Hanging lamps or chandeliers can be rigged with a pulley system for raising and lowering them, in the same way as hanging baskets.

While you are thinking of lighting the interior of your conservatory, give a thought to the exterior too. Lights on the patio or in the garden are not only useful if you are entertaining outside for part or all of the evening, but they also enable you to enjoy

ABOVE **Chandeliers of all sorts and sizes are widely available today, and you can find both modern and antique ones. If you buy an antique, make sure that it can be modified for electricity, if this has not already been done. Visit specialist lighting stores and antiques shops or go online to search out the perfect chandelier for your conservatory.**

RIGHT **This unusual Eastern-style lantern adds to the highly decorative conservatory dining room that has been built here on a flat-roofed extension. The room is north facing and has no need of blinds or curtains to provide shade, so the veneered table top is unlikely to suffer damage.**

the garden while you are inside the conservatory looking out.

Out of doors you could place LEDs around the edge of the patio or highlight steps leading to the garden, or even twist them around the trunk of a tree purely for decoration. Solar-powered lamps for lighting up paths or particular areas of the garden or patio are also available, but are most successful in regions with plenty of sunshine. If the power to your conservatory is largely solar generated, you will need to use LED or low-wattage long-life bulbs.

It is important that you inform your insurance company or broker that you are having a new conservatory built, because they may require you to take additional security measures. If you have an existing burglar-alarm system, you will need to talk to your security consultant about extending it to incorporate the new conservatory. If, like many people, you have located your conservatory at the back of your house, you would be advised to install a security lighting system to cover the area. Because a conservatory is an obvious point of entry for a burglar, it is sensible to use laminated or toughened glass and to install good locks on both the windows and doors.

ABOVE **A decorative white wall sculpture looks very good against the brickwork behind it and with ivy forming an attractive frame around it. Pieces of this sort can be found in a wide variety of places – you might even see something that you like when visiting another country and bring it home as a permanent reminder of a holiday.**

ABOVE **This conservatory lays the emphasis on plants rather than people, although it is simply furnished with a couple of comfortable wicker chairs in which to relax and enjoy the sun. A large Classical-style sculpture stands among the plants, the whiteness of its stone set off by all the green foliage.**

Sculpture

The inspiration for the tradition of housing a statue or two in the orangery or conservatory came originally from 18th-century Italy and was taken up by visiting grandees. Georgian orangeries were evidently used to display sculptures, placed here and there between the citrus trees in Versailles planters. As more people began to travel – to take their Grand Tour, for example – they brought home with them lovely pieces of sculpture made of marble, alabaster, and other types of stone. These precious objects were often taken into the conservatory for protection, rather than left outside.

Nowadays, most of us do not have the space for a very large piece, but sculpture comes in all shapes and sizes, and if you have an art object that you particularly like, a conservatory is an excellent place in which to display it to good advantage. If you are lucky enough to own a large statue or item of sculpture, you really need to think about where to position it fairly early on in your planning. Is it going to be freestanding, or are you going to place it on a plinth or pedestal? Is it going to look at its best facing into the sun, or with the sun behind it? Make sure that you allow it to be the centrepiece that

ABOVE You don't need to follow the style of the rest of your house in the way in which you decorate your conservatory. A great deal of furniture and artefacts from India, Indonesia, Thailand, Malaysia, and the Philippines is exported around the world, so it is easy to give a room an authentic Eastern feel, as seen in this example.

you want it to be, and don't mask it with chairs or other pieces of furniture. You will need to ensure, too, that you place it where it will not get in the way of anything else: you need to be able to move freely around it, to close the blinds, and open and close windows and doors without knocking it. Sculpture is often much more fragile than it looks – even cast iron will shatter if you drop it.

Statuary does not have to be placed on the floor, of course. It can be mounted on the wall or positioned on a shelf, possibly made of glass, or on a plinth or pedestal. And sculpture can be used in different ways, not merely for decoration. For example, two matching or complementary pieces could be used to mark an entryway, or to form a visual break in the room between two areas that are used in different ways.

You can hang a sculpture, if it is light enough, or if you have something sturdy to hang it from. There are all sorts of modern materials, such as resin, plaster, or even glazed dough, that are light enough to hang from a glazing bar. Remember that the larger the piece you want to display, the more careful you will have to be of its surroundings.

When you think of statuary, you may have in mind alabaster or marble figures, only partially covered by a few vine leaves, or naked, stone cherubs. Good examples of this type of Classical statuary look perfect in a similarly styled conservatory, but of course there are plenty of alternatives that will sit happily within other styles of interior. Generally speaking, a large piece of reproduction Greek or Roman statuary will look out of place in a very modern conservatory, while a contemporary, abstract piece will look strange in an otherwise traditional interior. Perhaps you have an artist friend that you could commission to make a sculpture specially for you and your conservatory? Visit art galleries, architectural salvage companies, auction rooms, and antiques shops to see what you can find. There are wonderful modern bronzes of birds and animals, and abstract sculpture can look fabulous in many different settings, too.

If you are already a collector, you might choose to decorate the whole conservatory to enhance your collection, whether that be of African tribal masks and figures or Indonesian shadow puppets. Perhaps your conservatory already has a theme – the beach,

ABOVE That this is a gardener's conservatory is easy to see from the sculptures that have been created from a mass of gardening tools – a simple idea that is both eye-catching and unusual. Sculptures can be wall mounted, as they are here, freestanding, or placed on shelving, a plinth, or a pedestal.

ABOVE RIGHT Lighting can double up as sculpture, as does this "Jack" light by British designer Tom Dixon. The piece has been carefully placed so that it can be viewed from within the house as well as the conservatory. Because the space has floor-to-ceiling glass walls, the light can also been seen from outside.

for example. In that case, you could look for sculptures to enhance the theme – seabirds, boats, even a large piece of driftwood that has been sculpted by the sea itself. Whether you have a sculpture already and design the rest of the room around it, or pick a piece or pieces that will suit the style of the room you already have, depends on you, your taste, and what you are happy to live with.

If your conservatory is primarily a place for growing plants rather than for entertaining people, it may be appropriate to display quite different pieces of sculpture to those that you would place in your sitting room. A marble or alabaster head looking out from behind the foliage, perhaps, or a bronze bird stalking through the undergrowth, or an animal of some sort – any of these could look great. If you grow a mass of exotic tropical plants and palms you might find a sculpture of some equally exotic animal or bird that would suit your plants perfectly. On the other hand, if you have a large number of cacti, you might be able to find a piece of abstract sculpture made in sandstone that would form a complementary focal point.

Water features

A fountain or water feature of some description is often thought to be highly desirable in conservatories as well as outdoors. However, as with other finishing touches, a water feature is something that you will need to decide upon during the early planning stage of your conservatory because you will need a water supply and, most likely, an electrical socket nearby for a small electric pump.

Fountains are available in many styles, and so too are wall-mounted Neptunes, roaring lions, or grotesque figures with water spouting from their open mouths. If you do not want a separate pool, a cast-iron, glazed ceramic, or cast-stone wall fountain might be worth considering. These are quite practical and need not take up much space, but call for expert installation. Alternatively, you could find a specialist designer to make you a modern water feature, such as a wall of water, which can look wonderful.

You could decide to leave a space for a pond in the floor, have a raised pond built, or even consider having a pond made that is half inside and half outside the conservatory, so that fish can swim freely between the two areas. If the water level is correctly measured,

ABOVE LEFT Water features and fountains do not have to take up much space. This one is located in the corner of the conservatory and is surrounded by plants that disguise its edge somewhat. There are many sizes and styles of wall fountain available, in ceramic, stone, and terra cotta as well as iron.

ABOVE RIGHT The eye is drawn toward the white stone of the water feature, which shows up clearly against the wall behind it. The cherubic figures playing and the water arcing out of the fountain make an attractive sight, and the wavy edge of the bowl mimics the shapes of the many and varied plants that surround the fountain.

no gap will exist between the edge of the glass and the water, and no draft will spoil your enjoyment inside. Although condensation will be inevitable in hot weather, it need not be a problem, providing that you have good ventilation.

If you are very good at DIY, you might decide to make a small pond yourself, but you could equally well put in a bamboo or ceramic water feature. These are available even in tiny sizes and can look charming. A Japanese-style bamboo water feature makes a soothing *tock-tock* sound as the water runs through and between the hollow canes causing them to knock against one another.

Many different styles and types of statue are available for use in a pond, some of which are integral to the design, but even if you decide not to opt for a fountain, you could add a statue to a pond or other water feature. A nymph or cherub could be placed on a plinth in the middle, or, if the pond is located at the base of a solid wall, you could leave enough space behind it for a plinth upon which to place a statue or a sculpture.

A water feature is a lovely addition to a conservatory – and the peaceful sound of trickling water is a magical antidote to the stress of a hectic day's work. You might think of adding discreetly disguised lighting – white, coloured, or a combination of the two – around your pool or fountain. Imagine relaxing there in the evening, glass in hand, soothing music playing in the background, while you watch sparkling droplets of water flash through the air.

LEFT This is a splendid Moroccan conservatory, designed in a traditional way in vivid blue with decorative tiling at the rear. There is obviously enough humidity to keep the banana plants happy, and the cacti appear to be thriving as well. The blue pool, fountain, and wall are reminiscent of warm climates in a way that cool stone shades rarely are.

6

Freestanding glasshouses

A freestanding glasshouse is relatively unusual in this day and age – it is truly a luxury item and is generally suitable only for a property that is surrounded by a fairly large garden. However, if you are fortunate enough to live in such a property, you might be able to have the best of both worlds – an attached conservatory and a stand-alone glass palace. The rest of us can admire and dream!

PREVIOUS PAGES This traditional glasshouse has been positioned against the rear garden wall and has trees growing both behind and beside it, giving shade in the summer, when it is mainly used. Plants can be overwintered here, and when all doors to the central bay are opened in warm weather, it makes a lovely, outdoor summer room.

LEFT A glasshouse built in the style of a traditional orangery stands at the end of a swathe of perfectly cut grass, giving a beautiful view back toward the main house. It is built of stone and wood, with the colour of the stone carefully chosen to complement that of the house. This would be a wonderful venue for a cocktail party.

A freestanding glasshouse may seem to be virtually the same thing as a conservatory attached to a house, but the reality is very different. A freestanding glasshouse has a different function, because, apart from anything else, you have to leave your house and walk across the garden to reach it. It might be positioned in order to hide something unattractive. In the past, wealthy landowners sometimes built orangeries to block the view of the bare trunks of a small grove, a working area, such as a vegetable garden, or the living quarters of the gardening staff.

Orangeries were being built in France and Italy by the middle of the 1500s, but these stone buildings were exactly what their name implied – houses built for the protection of tender orange trees during the winter. The fashion for adding conservatories to middle-class homes did not encompass freestanding glasshouses, which remained the preserve of the wealthy. Sometimes glasshouses would be built separately from the house but attached to an existing garden wall, but they were largely used for growing vines and other plants, in much the same way as we would use greenhouses nowadays.

Glasshouses today serve various functions. There are attractive ones for growing plants and even more beautiful ones that are really for the enjoyment of people, but

OPPOSITE LEFT This glasshouse on a roof in central London is a lovely sight. Lit at night, as it is here, to give a dramatic view of the lush flowers and foliage within, it is a reminder to all who see it that a different world exists outside the city. Here the gardener can wander about in a another world, instantly escaping from the stress of a busy city life.

OPPOSITE RIGHT An original Victorian glasshouse, in Cornwall, England. In this case its emphasis is very much on growing plants, and it provides a wonderful point of focus for a traditional walled garden.

that also protect the plants growing within. A glasshouse might be built in order to enable the owners to enjoy a view that is invisible from the house – a lake or a particular area of the grounds perhaps – or it could house a swimming pool or a games room. But whatever its use – and unlike a conservatory – it will not feel purely like an extension of your home.

Many glasshouses are unheated, relying instead on very good insulation by the glass and masonry to minimize the chill, and so receive most use during warmer weather. Heating was brought into the glasshouse during the 1600s, and by the 1800s, many different techniques were being employed, using complicated systems of stoves, boilers, and pipes.

Today, the cost of running power and water out to the glasshouse will be considerable, and the problem of heating, if you plan to have any, has to be thought about as well. You will have to discuss heating matters with your architect or suppliers. Would it be best to install a dedicated system, involving a separate boiler house for the glasshouse, or should you run electricity from the main house? Electricity will be the easy and cheap to install, but expensive to run. Or perhaps, depending upon where you live, you could run a solar- or wind-powered system.

LEFT A geodesic dome is just one of the radically different shapes that are available today. Spectacular though it is, a dome like this does have its difficulties: the space around the edge is largely unusable because of its limited height, for example. However, as you can see, there is enough room in this one for a table and chairs as well as for a few plants.

BELOW A six-sided glasshouse, where old meets new – Victorian styling is accompanied by tinted glass to prevent the sun from overheating the interior. A tiled path connects the building to the main house for ease of access.

Styles, uses, and materials

If we can assume, for the sake of argument, that money is no object, then you can have a glasshouse built to almost any design you choose, from a traditional orangery, constructed in brick or stone, or the more usual Victorian styles – wooden framed and built on a dwarf wall, to an ultra-modern geodesic dome. The style you choose will depend, to some extent, upon the use you are going to make of the place. A separate glasshouse to accommodate a swimming pool will probably be quite different in shape and size to one in which you plan to relax with a drink and a book, for example.

The idea of having a swimming pool can be extremely tempting, but in colder, northern climes, it really needs to be indoors if you want to be able to use it all year round. Some houses have indoor swimming pools, but it would be so much more pleasant to have a separate building made largely of glass for your pool that would give you the sense of being outside even in the depths of winter. During the summer months, you would be able to open the doors all the way round so that you really would be swimming in the fresh air.

ABOVE **This is a very well-constructed, aluminium-framed botanical glasshouse. The simple design is pleasing to the eye, and the building is large enough to house a variety of palms and other striking-looking plants. The temperature within is automatically controlled, so when you have finished the gardening, you can sit down and enjoy the environment.**

Another possible use of a glasshouse is as a recreation or games room. You could build one to house a full-sized billiards table or a table-tennis table, or even make it into a room in which to hold bridge parties – all of these hobbies require a reasonable amount of space. A glasshouse can also make a pefect studio for an artist or sculptor – there is plenty of light, you can be left to work in peace, and because you will no doubt have a wonderful view, it will probably give you inspiration as well.

If you are running a large household and are surrounded by people most of the time, you probably crave some time to yourself. A separate glasshouse can give you somewhere to go and escape everyday stress. Instead of hiding away in your bedroom, you could take yourself off to your glasshouse for an hour or two, leaving strict instructions that you are to be left alone, and sit down and look at the view, or read, or meditate.

Entertaining or dining in a separate glasshouse requires more planning than in a conservatory that adjoins the house. All the food and drink will have to be brought over from the kitchen, but if the party is informal you can rope in other members of the family or guests to help you carry things. Cold food is obviously easier to organize than hot food, but you will have electricity in the glasshouse and you could always buy an electrically heated trolley to keep everything hot. If you hold a more formal party, you could hire caterers to help and/or waiting staff to hand around drinks and canapés.

Furniture

The type of furniture that you choose for your glasshouse will depend on whether or not you are going to heat it. For many people, the prospect of having to heat the place all winter is a step too far, and they decide to think of a glasshouse as a summer space. Even if you do not install central heating, however, you will want to run electricity from the house. Make sure that you have a few wall sockets, so that you can plug in an electric heater if you want to. You will also be able to have a few individual lamps then, too.

Furnishing an unheated glasshouse needs careful consideration: your options will be more limited than when furnishing a conservatory, particularly if you live in a cold climate and may therefore be using the space for less than half the year. In these circumstances, your glasshouse will be left alone to the damp and the cold, apart from when you drop in to water your plants, and your furniture needs to be able to withstand such conditions.

You will need strong furniture that requires little maintenance, and garden furniture made of hardwood derived from a sustainable source would be a sensible solution. Oak or teak are obvious choices, and both mellow pleasantly. Cast- or wrought-iron furniture are

ABOVE This lovely cool, Classical glasshouse is intended for use as a place to entertain guests as well as somewhere quiet to sit and read or just relax. Underfloor heating is a good option for a glasshouse of this size; it allows wooden and cane furniture, which would suffer in an unheated space, to be kept here permanently.

PREVIOUS PAGES It is important to think carefully about the placement of your glasshouse and how it will fit in with its surroundings. The glasshouse shown on the left was placed deliberately to make the most of the view of the lily pond that stretches out in front of it and is made in part from reclaimed bricks that match those of the garden wall. The one on the right is more modern in style and has been built in conjunction with a swimming pool.

RIGHT This hexagonal, wood-framed glasshouse is heated during the winter, so that it can be used year round. This enables the owners to have wooden and upholstered furniture within it and to keep plates and table linen permanently in the dresser at the rear. Wooden furniture of this sort would not be suitable in an unheated glasshouse.

other alternatives, while contemporary furniture for the modern glasshouse is also available in steel and in high-tech materials. You will probably want seat cushions, and they will have to be brought back into the house when the summer is over because they will become dank and unpleasant if left in the glasshouse over the winter.

If you decide to centrally heat your glasshouse all year round, bear in mind that they generally look better without radiators. Think about installing underfloor heating, powered by electricity, oil, or gas, instead. Alternatively, you could have hot-air vents, with decorative grilles, if this suits the style you are after. Providing the room is kept at a reasonable temperature, you can fit it with the same kind of furniture you would have in a conservatory. However, bear in mind that the sun can dry out and bleach furniture and fabrics, so provide adequate protection with blinds.

You may also want to include a dresser or storage of some description, so that you can keep tablecloths, glasses, odd items of cutlery such as a sharp knife, a bottle opener, and possibly a few plates to hand. These could all be brought back indoors during the winter or you could just bring in the linen. Don't forget that you will need to have a tap installed nearby so that you don't have to carry a watering can or hosepipe around and so that you will be able to wipe the table-top without having to go back to the house. Remember that there is no point in making the investment in a glasshouse if using it makes more work for you – it should be a magical, luxurious place, not a chore.

Planting

The plants you can grow in your glasshouse will also depend to a large extent on whether or not it is heated. Work out what the minimum temperature will be and plant accordingly. Do some research into the plants that will do well in your glasshouse by reading books and taking advice from good garden centres and conservatory-gardening experts.

Is this a space where plants will take centre stage, or is it primarily a room in which to relax? Consider, too, the style you have in mind for the room as a whole. If you are aiming for a traditional style, then the plants you choose will be quite different from those you may want in a radical, modern glasshouse.

If you can guarantee that the minimum interior temperature will not fall below 5°C (41°F), you could have a formal, Classical style of planting, with citrus trees in Versailles tubs arranged at intervals around the walls, possibly interspersed with bay trees, perhaps clipped into the shape of a ball or an animal.

Abutilon, a South American shrub with lovely bell-shaped flowers, will survive a cold winter – just keep it relatively dry, and it will come back to life in the spring. (If you are

ABOVE **This large Victorian-style glasshouse calls to mind the glasshouses in botanical gardens such as Kew and New York. Because of its size it is able to offer an entrance on every side. This is particularly convenient when moving and maintaining very large plants.**

nervous about its chances of survival in winter, take a few cuttings in the late summer and overwinter them indoors.) *A.* x *suntense*, deciduous and with large, pale-mauve flowers, is a frost-hardy hybrid. Some species of acacia are suitable, too – their bobbles of yellow flowers appearing in early spring are a hopeful sign of better weather to come.

There are many suitable climbers, too, if they are more your style – bougainvillea, for example, can withstand quite low temperatures, although it is generally thought of as a warm-weather plant. It will lose its leaves in the winter and need little water during that time. *Campsis* is a genus of very exotic-looking, deciduous climbers with racemes of large, showy trumpet-shaped flowers and pretty leaves. These plants can be contained in a pot, but will grow much bigger if planted in the ground. A vine would, in time, provide some summer shade in the glasshouse and can be grown in a pot. Alternatively, you could plant it outside and leave a space in the dwarf wall to bring it through into the glasshouse.

If you have a modern, floor-to-ceiling glass building, or a geodesic dome, you will probably want a few striking, architectural plants. Palms are the obvious answer – several species can cope with low temperatures. Check that the plants have been raised by the nursery, or acclimatized for at least one year before you buy them. Other options include *Butia capitata*, the Brazilian jelly palm, which has lovely arching, feathery blue-grey leaves, or *Chamaerops humilis*, the European fan palm. *Phormium tenax*, the New Zealand flax, which is smaller than the palms, would also be a good choice, and some of its cultivars have beautiful leaves of bronze and purple, or stripes of cream and red. These are all plants that keep their leaves year round – merely cut old leaves back to the stem.

ABOVE **The showy yellow blooms and variegated leaves of an** *Abutilon* **arch over the intense red flowers of** *Salvia Coccinea.* **Both are tender perennials from South America but can thrive in a glasshouse.**

RIGHT **Bougainvillea and plumbago scramble up the wall of a glasshouse. These two plants provide both spectacular flowers in the summer and a useful backdrop of foliage in the winter, as they are evergreen.**

ABOVE What a splendid idea it was to build a glasshouse in the middle of this formally laid-out knot garden. Whether it is lit by electricity, candlelight, or just moonlight, this glasshouse is a lovely to look at, and the dedicated heating system enables it to be enjoyed even in the depths of winter.

OPPOSITE This is an extraordinarily grandiose glasshouse that could only really be suitable for the most spectacular of country-house estates. Beautifully lit, the dome and lantern, with its high-level ventilation, look awesome, and the whole building has an aura that is both exciting and inviting. This would be a perfect place for a romantic dinner party.

A–Z of suitable plants

Botanical name	Common name

MIXED PLANTING

Botanical name	Common name
Amaryllis	
Arctotis	African daisy
Azalea	
Begonia	
Crocus	
Fuchsia	
Hedera	Ivy
Hyacinth	
Impatiens	Busy Lizzie
Mesembryanthemum	
Narcissus	Daffodil
Pansy	
Pelargonium	
Petunia	
Primula	
Tulipa	Tulip
Viola	

CLIMBERS

Botanical name	Common name
Allemanda cathartica	Golden trumpet
Araujia sericofera	Cruel plant
Bougainvillea	
Canarina canariensis	Canary Islands bellflower
Clerodendrum thomsoniae	Bleeding heart vine
Clianthus puniceus	Lobster claw
Cobaea scandens	Cup-and-saucer plant
Gloriosa superba	Glory lily
Hardenbergia violacea	
Hoya carnosa	Wax plant
Ipomoea	Morning glory
Jasminum	Jasmine
Lapageria rosea	Chilean bellflower
Pandora jasminoides	Bower plant
Passiflora	Passionflower
Philodendron scandens	Sweetheart plant
Plumbago auriculata	Plumbago
Plumeria rubra	Frangipani
Pyrostegia venusta	
Rosa banksiae 'Lutea'	Yellow Lady Banks' rose
Rosa 'Maréchal Niel'	

Senecio tamoides	
Stephanotis floribunda	Madagascar jasmine
Thunbergia alata	Black-eyed Susan vine
Thunbergia grandiflora	Blue trumpet vine

TRAILERS

Botanical name	Common name
Aeschynanthus radicans	Lipstick vine
Asparagus densiflorus	Asparagus fern
Begonia	
Callisia	
Campanula	Bellflower
Chlorophytum comosum	Spider plant
Codonanthe	
Columnea gloriosa	Goldfish plant
Episcia dianthiflora	Lace-flower vine
Fuchsia	
Hedera	Ivy
Hoya bella	
Lobelia	
Lotus berthelotii	
Pelargonium	
Piper ornatum	Celebes pepper
Plectranthus	
Saxifraga	
Schlumbergera bridgesii	Christmas cactus
Senecio macroglossus 'Variegatus'	
Stenotaphrum	
Tradescantia	Wandering Jew or Inch plant
Tropaeolum	Nasturtium

EXOTICS

Botanical name	Common name
Aechmea fasciata	Urn plant
Allamanda schottii	Bush allamanda
Alocasia macrorrhiza	Giant elephant's ear
Brugmansia	Angel's trumpet
Clivia miniata	Kaffir lily
Guzmania	
Heliconia rostrata	Lobster claw
Hibiscus	
Orchids	
Pavonia multiflora	

Protea cynaroides	King protea
Stephanotis floribunda	Madagascar jasmine
Strelitzia reginae	Bird-of-paradise plant
Thunbergia mysorensis	Clock vine
Zantedeschia aethiopica	Calla lily

DESERT PLANTS: CACTI AND SUCCULENTS

Aeonium arboreum	House leek tree
Agave americana	American aloe
Agave americana 'Mediopicta'	
Aporocactus	
Borzicactus aureispinus	
Ceropegia	
Cleistocactus	
Crassula ovata	Money plant
Echeveria secunda	
Echinocactus	
Epiphyllum	Orchid cactus
Espostoa	
Euphorbia milii	Crown of thorns
Hatiora rosea	Easter cactus
Kalanchoe	
Lepismium	
Lithops	
Lobivia backebergia	
Mammilaria	
Opuntia phaeacantha	Prickly pear
Rebutia	
Schlumbergera bridgesii	Christmas cactus
Sedum morganianum	Burro's tail

FRUIT, VEGETABLES, AND HERBS

Apricot
Citrus
Fig
Grape
Melon
Nectarine
Olive
Peach
Pineapple

Pomegranate
Aubergine
Chilli pepper
Cucumber (not with melon – the melon aphid is one of the chief agents in transmitting cucumber mosaic virus)
Okra
Pepper
Tomato
Basil
Chervil
Chive
Coriander
Ginger
Marjoram
Mint
Parsley
Sorrel
Tarragon

OVERWINTERING

Azalea	
Cacti	
Cyclamen	
Heathers	
Hippeastrum	Amaryllis
Solanum capsicastrum	Winter cherry
Spring bulbs	

ARCHITECTURAL

Brugmansia	Angel's trumpet
Calathea zebrina	Zebra plant
Cordyline	Cabbage tree
Cycas revoluta	Sago palm
Ensete ventricosum	Banana plant
Fatsia japonica	Paperplant
Ficus benjamina	Weeping fig
Ficus benjamina 'Variegata'	Variegated weeping fig
Ficus elastica	Rubber plant
Guzmania lingulata	
Guzmania musaica	
Hibiscus rosa-sinensis	

Hippeastrum	Amaryllis
Hoya carnosa	Wax plant
Justicia	
Monstera deliciosa	Swiss-cheese plant
Nerium oleander	
Philodendron	
Phoenix canariensis	Canary Islands date palm
Sansevieria trifasciata	Mother-in-law's tongue
Schefflera actinophylla	Queensland umbrella tree
Trachycarpus fortunei	Windmill palm
Yucca elephantipes	Spineless yucca
Yucca elephantipes 'Variegata'	Variegated spineless yucca

WATER GARDEN

Butomus umbellatus	Flowering rush
Caltha palustris	Marsh marigold
Canna	
Cyperus papyrus	Egyptian papyrus
Iris	
Lysichiton	
Marsilea	
Nelumbo	Lotus
Nymphaea	Water lily
Onoclea sensibilis	Sensitive fern
Oryza sativa	Rice
Pistia stratiotes	Water lettuce
Ranunculus aquatilis	Water buttercup
Schoenoplectus lacustris subsp. *tabernaemontana*	
Xanthosoma nigrum	

LOW MAINTENANCE

FERNS

Adiantum raddianum	Delta maidenhair fern
Asparagus densiflorus	Asparagus fern
Asplenium nidus	Bird's-nest fern
Blechnum gibbum	Miniature tree fern
Cyathea australis	Rough tree fern
Cyrtomium falcatum	Holly fern
Davallia canariensis	Hare's-foot fern
Nephrolepis exaltata	Boston fern

Phlebodium aureum	
Platycerium bifurcatum	Common staghorn fern
Pteris	

CARNIVOROUS

Darlingtonia californica	Cobra lily
Dionaea muscipula	Venus fly trap
Drosera	Sundew
Heliamphora	Sun pitcher
Nepenthes	Pitcher plant
Pinguicula	Butterwort
Sarracenia	Pitcher plant

Selected suppliers

UK

Amdega Ltd
Faverdale
Darlington DL3 0PW
Tel: 0800 591 523

Apropos Tectonic Ltd
Greenside House
Richmond Street
Ashton-Under-Lyne OL6 7ES
Tel: 0870 777 0326
www.apropos-tectonic.com

B&Q
Branches nationwide
Tel: 0845 850 0175
www.diy.com

David Salisbury
Bennett Road
Highbridge TA9 4PW
Tel: 0844 800 8808
www.davidsalisbury.com

Direct Conservatories 4U
Suite 27 Silk House
Park Green
Macclesfield SK11 7QJ
Tel: 0845 058 6001
www.directconservatories4u.co.uk

Fawsley
c/o Durabuild Glazed Structures Ltd
Carlton Road
Coventry CV6 7FL
Tel: 024 7666 9166
www.fawsley.com

Glass Houses Ltd
Barnsbury Street
Islington

London N1 1PW
Tel: 020 7607 6071
www.glasshouses.com

Hartley Botanic
Greenside House
Richmond Street
Ashton Under Lyne OL6 7ES
Tel: 0870 777 0320
www.hartleybotanic.co.uk

James Harcourt
Hockley Court
Stratford Road
Hockley Heath
Solihull B94 6NW
Tel: 0870 241 6337.
www.jamesharcourt.co.uk

Jeremy Uglow
Unit 5 A–D
Blacknest Works
Blacknest GU34 4PW
Tel: 01420 520009
www.jeremyuglow.com

Machin Conservatories
Faverdale
Darlington DL3 0P
Tel: 01325 360776
www.machin-conservatories.com

Marston & Langinger Ltd
192 Ebury Street
London SW1V 8UP
Tel: 020 7881 5700
www.marston-and-langinger.com

Opus Conservatories
The Red House
10 Market Square
Old Amersham HP7 0DQ

Tel: 01494 445558
www.opusconservatories.co.uk

Prime Oak Buildings Limited
Whitehouse Farm
Whitehouse Lane
Swindon DY3 4PE
Tel: 01384 296611
www.primeoak.co.uk

Priory Conservatories
50 Albert Road North
Reigate RH2 9EL
Tel: 01737 221296
www.priory-lifestyle.com

Town & Country Masterworks in Glass
61 Lambeth Walk
London SE11 6DX
Tel: 020 7091 0621
www.townandcountryuk.com

Trombé Conservatories
307 Old Street
London EC1V 9LA
Tel: 020 7684 1065
www.trombe.co.uk

Vale Garden Houses
Londonthorpe Road
Grantham NG31 9SJ
Tel: 01476 564433
www.valegardenhouses.com

Westbury Conservatories Ltd
Martels
High Easter Road
Barnston CM6 1NA
Tel: 01371 876567
www.conservatoriesbywestbury.com

North America

Brady-Built of New England
160 Southbridge Street
Auburn, MA 01501
Tel: 508 798 2600
www.bradyrooms.com

British Conservatories
Temple, PA 19560
Tel: 800 566 6360
www.britishrose.com

Classic Conservatories
Mountainside, NJ
Tel: 800 435 1188
www.classicconservatories.com

Creative Structures Conservatories
420 Station Road
Quakertown, PA 18951
Tel: 800 873 3966
www.creativeconservatories.com

Four Seasons Sunrooms
5005 Veterans Memorial Highway,
Holbrook, NY 11741
Tel: 631 563 4000
www.four-seasons.com

Freeport Conservatory Company
180 US Route One
Freeport, ME 04032
Tel: 207 865 0899
www.freeportconservatories.com

Gorrell Grand Additions
1380 Wayne Avenue
Indiana, PA 15701
Tel: 888 822 2485
www.grandadditions.com

K2 (USA) Conservatory Systems
Airport Technical Center
136 West 64th Street,
Holland, M1 49423
Tel: 616 796 9940
www.canterburyconservatory.com

Town & Country Masterworks in Glass
North American Sales and Design
1475 West Foster Avenue
Chicago, IL 60640
Tel: 773 506 8000
www.townandcountryus.com

Monarch Conservatories
4 Scarlett Line
Hillsdale, Ontario L0L 1V0
Canada
Tel: 705 8351558
www.monarchconservatory.com

New England Conservatories
4 Moriarty Road
Ware, MA 1082
Tel: 413 967 9093
www.newenglandconservatories.net

Patio Enclosures
720 East Highland Road
Macedonia, OH 44056
Tel: 800 468 0720
www.patioenclosuresinc.com

Renaissance Conservatories
132 Ashmore Drive
Leola, PA 17540
Tel: 800 882 4657
www.renaissance-online.com

Royal American Sunrooms &
Conservatories LLC
2520 Colby Ave

Everett, WA 98201-2990,
Tel: 206 850 3600
www.royalamericansunrooms.com

Seattle Sun Systems
1701 1st Avenue
S. Seattle, WA 98199
Tel: 206 3432822
www.seattlesun.com

Solar Innovations
East Rosebud Road
Myerstown, PA 17067
Tel: 800 618 0669
www.solarinnovations.com

Sunroom Design Company
13 Highland Street
East Hartford, CT 06108
Tel: 877 766 7297
www.sunroomdesign.com

Sunspaces
407 132nd Avenue, NE, #7
Bellevue, WA 98005
Tel: 425 454 4336
www.sun-spaces.com

Tanglewood Conservatories
15 Engerman Avenue
Denton, MD 21629
Tel: 800 229 2925
www.tanglewoodconservatories.com

Westview Products
1350 SE Shelton Street
Dallas, OR 97338
Tel: 800 203 7557
www.westviewproducts.com

Index

Acknowledgments

Mitchell Beazley would like to acknowledge and thank all the conservatory and glass house suppliers, photographers and architects who have provided images for use in this book.

Special thanks to Alan West at Trombé, and Alicia Moyer at Solar Innovations, Inc, who provided plans and diagrams.

Key: a above, b below, c centre, l left, r right

1 Interior Archive/Fritz von der Schulenberg/design: Nina Campbell, 2 Interior Archive/Christopher Simon Sykes, 5ra as24, 5rc see 44, 5rb see 74, 5la see 115, 5lc see 160, 5lb see 182, 6 Corbis/Clay Perry, 7 Bridgeman Art Library/Yale Center for British Art, Paul Mellon Collection, USA, 8 Art Archive/Dagli Orti, 9 Corbis/Lee Snider, 10 Bridgeman Art Library/Charles Plante Fine Arts/Private Collection, 11l Hulton Archive/Getty Images, 11r Hulton Archive/Stringer/Getty Images, 12 Paul Archer Design, 13 Arcaid/Alan Weintraub/architect: Mickey Muennig, 14 Amdega, 16a Four Seasons Sunrooms, 16b Harpur Garden Library/Jerry Harpur/design: David Pearson, 17 Vale Garden Houses, 18 Red Cover/Grant Govier, 19 Nicola Browne/design: Ross Palmer, 20 Westbury Conservatories, 21l courtesy of Solar Innovations, Inc, 21r Garden Picture Library/Ron Sutherland/design: Duane Paul Design Team, 22-23 Westbury Conservatories, 24 Garden Picture Library/Ron Sutherland, 25 Glass Houses, 26 Richard Bloom, 27ar Wintergarten Fachverband, 27bl Harpur Garden Library/Jerry Harpur, 28 Verandas Raoul TNN, 29a Richmond Oak Ltd, 29b Apropos Tectonic Ltd, 30 Town & Country, 31 Harpur Garden Library/Marcus Harpur/design: Ferrand, 32 Square Garden, 33a Baumann, 33b Heritage Conservatories, 34 Garden Picture Library/John Miller/design: Marin Miles, 35 Harpur Garden Library/Jerry Harpur/design: Westbury Conservatories, 36 Square Garden, 37a Red Cover/Hugh Palmer, 37 Direct Conservatories 4 U, 38, 39 Wintergarten Fachverband, 40l & r, 41 Trombé Conservatories, 42 Garden Picture Library/Marie O'Hara, 44-45 Fawsley, 45 Apropos Tectonic Ltd, 46 Machin, 47 Red Cover/Dan Duchars, 48 Wintergarten Fachverband, 49l David Salisbury, 49r Town & Country, 50a Harpur Garden Library/Jerry Harpur/design: Tom Shanley, 50b Glass Houses, 51a & b Four Seasons Sunrooms, 52 Verandas Raoul TNN, 53l Four Seasons Sunrooms, 53r Garden Picture Library/Ron Sutherland/design: Duane Paul Design Team, 54-55 Marston & Langinger Ltd, 56a Glass Houses, 56b Garden Picture Library/Friedrich Strauss, 57 Vale Garden Houses, 58 Garden Picture Library/John Miller/Ettington Park Hotel, 59 Garden Picture Library/Roy Asser, 60a Quantal Conservatory Roofing System, 60b Garden Picture Library/Ron Sutherland, 61 David Salisbury, 62 Square Garden, 63a Vale Garden Houses, 63b Harpur Garden Library/Jerry Harpur/design: Peter Causer, Roja Dove Brighton, 64 Town & Country, 65 Andrew Lawson, 66l Town & Country, 66 Glass Houses, 67 Alamy/Elizabeth Whiting & Associates, 68l Fawsley, 68r Town & Country, 69 Oak Leaf Conservatories, 70 David Salisbury, 71l Guy Bouchet, 71r Harpur Garden Library/Marcus Harpur/Bill Taubman, USA, 72 Steven Wooster/Bosvigo House, Cornwall, 74 Garden Picture Library/Suzie Gibbons, 75 Interior Archive/Fritz von der Schulenberg, 76 Derek St Romaine, 77 Nicola Stocken Tomkins/RHS Wisley, 78l Interior Archive/Fritz von der Schulenburg, 78r Rob Whitworth/RHS Chelsea Flower Show, 79 Eric Crichton, 80a Steven Wooster/The Old Vicarage, Norfolk, 80b Nicola Stocken Tomkins, 81 Harpur Garden Library/Jerry Harpur/Armand, Chiswick, 82 Eric Crichton, 83l Derek St Romaine/West Dean Gardens, Singleton, Sussex, 83r Steven Wooster, 84 Steven Wooster, 85l Eric Crichton, 85r Vale Garden Houses, 86 Garden Picture Library/Howard Rice, 87 Interior Archive/Fritz von der Schulenburg/design: Rosemary Verey, 88-89 Harpur Garden Library/Jerry Harpur/design: Maggie Gundry, 90a Octopus Publishing Group/Steven Wooster, 90c Octopus Publishing Group/Michael Boys, 90b Steven Wooster/The Plantsman Nursery, 91a Octopus Publishing Group/Michael Boys, 91c Octopus Publishing Group/Jerry Harpur, 91 b Steven Wooster/The Old Vicarage Garden, Norfolk, 92l Garden Picture Library/Botanica/Tim Street-Porter, 92r Interior Archive/Fritz von der Schulenburg, 93 Harpur Garden Library/Jerry Harpur, 94 Garden World Images/C Fairweather, 95 Nicola Stocken Tomkins, 96a & c Octopus Publishing /JamesYoung, 96b Nicola Stocken Tomkins, 97a Andrew Lawson, 97b John Glover, 97c S & O Mathews, 98 Garden World Images/C Fairweather, 99a Octopus Publishing Group/Jerry Harpur, 99bl John Glover, 99br S & O Mathews, 100l Steven Wooster, 100r Octopus Publishing Group/Michael Boys, 101l Octopus Publishing Group, 101r Sunniva Harte/J Tunstall, 101b S & O Mathews, 102 Garden Picture Library/Friedrich Strauss, 103 Garden World Images/P Hart, 104a Harpur Garden Library/Jerry Harpur/Vernon Stratton, 104b Heritage Conservatories, 105 Vale Garden Houses, 106-7 Octopus Publishing Group/Steven Wooster, 108 Garden Picture Library/Christopher Gallagher, 109 Eric Crichton, 110 Rob Whitworth/design: Alan Titchmarsh, 111l Alamy/Garden Picture Library/John Glover, 11lr Westbury Conservatories, 114 Narratives/Jan Baldwin/design: Grant White, 115a Andreas von Einsiedel, 115b Garden Picture Library/Ron Sutherland, 116 Andrew Lawson /Bosvigo House, Cornwall, 117 Red Cover/Kim Sayer; 118, 119 Vale Garden Houses, 120 Westbury Conservatories, 121l Holloways, 121b The Cotswold Company, 122 Alcoa Architecture, 123 Holloways, 124 Corbis/Massimo Listri, 125 Vale Garden Houses, 126-7 Westbury Conservatories, 128 Andrew Lawson, 129 Amdega, 130 Andrew Lawson/RHS Chelsea 2001, 131 Red Cover/Douglas Gibb, 132-133 Harpur Garden Library/Jerry Harpur/Park Farm, 134,135a Trombé Conservatories, 135b Red Cover/Johnny Bouchier, 136 Alamy/Elizabeth Whiting Associates, 137a Glass Houses, 137b Narratives/Jan Baldwin/design: Christopher Healey, 138 Red Cover/Andrew Twort, 139 Marston & Langinger, 140a Wintergarten Facverband eV, 140b Clive Nichols/Lisette Pleasance, 141 Harpur Garden Library/Jerry Harpur, 142 Narratives/Jan Baldwin/design: Grant White, 143a & b Square Garden, 144 Garden Picture Library/Tommy Candler, 145 Garden Picture Library/Paul Windsor, 146 Mainstream/Ray Main, 148 Appeal Conservatory Blinds Ltd, 149l K2, 149r Marson & Langinger, 150 Square Garden, 151 Photolibrary.com/Photononstop, 152a Red Cover/Grey Crawford, 152b Harpur Garden Library/Jerry Harpur, 153a Appeal Conservatory Blinds Ltd, 153b Wintergarten Fachverband, 154 Vale Garden Houses, 155a, b Appeal Conservatory Blinds Ltd, 156 Apropos Tectonic Ltd, 157, 158 Amdega, 159a Andreas von Einsiedel, 159b Andrew Lawson/design: Jacqueline Geddes, 160 Harpur Garden Library/Jerry Harpur, 161 Marston & Langinger, 162 Holloways, 162r Red Cover/Hugh Palmer, 163 Nicola Browne/design: Sue Firth, 164 Red Cover/Hugh Palmer, 165 View/Philip Bier, 166l Interior Archive/Fritz von der Schulenberg, 166r Vale Garden Houses, 167 Eric Crichton, 168-9 The Garden Collection/Liz Eddison, 170, 172 Glass Houses, 173l Machin, 173r Andrew Lawson/Bosvigo House, Cornwall, 174a Solardome, registered trademark of Solardome Industries Ltd, 174b K2, 175 Hartley Botanic,176 The Garden Collection/Marie O'Hara, 177 Marston & Langinger, 178, 179 Glass Houses, 180 Town & Country, 181l Harpur Garden Library/Jerry Harpur/design: Maggie Gundry, 181r Nicola Stocken Tomkins, 182 Apropos Tectonic Ltd, 183 Oak Leaf Conservatories.